Community Engagement and Investment

Community Engagement and Investment

Alan S. Gutterman

BUSINESS EXPERT PRESS

Leader in applied, concise business books

Community Engagement and Investment

Cover design by Charlene Kronstedt

Interior design by Exeter Premedia Services Private Ltd., Chennai, India

First published in 2021 by
Business Expert Press, LLC
222 East 46th Street, New York, NY 10017
www.businessexpertpress.com

ISBN-13: 978-1-95334-990-3 (paperback)
ISBN-13: 978-1-95334-991-0 (e-book)

Business Expert Press Environmental and Social Sustainability for Business Advantage Collection

Collection ISSN: 2327-333X (print)
Collection ISSN: 2327-3348 (electronic)

First edition: 2021

10 9 8 7 6 5 4 3 2 1

Description

Sustainability is about the long-term well-being of society, an issue that encompasses a wide range of aspirational targets including ending poverty and hunger; ensuring healthy lives, and promoting well-being for all; ensuring inclusive and equitable quality education and promoting lifelong learning opportunities for all; and promoting sustained, inclusive, and sustainable economic growth, full and productive employment and decent work for all. Clearly the challenges associated with pursuing the goals are daunting and for most businesses, it may be difficult for them to see how they can play a meaningful role in address them. While it is common for "society" to be identified as an organizational stakeholder, the reality is that one company cannot, acting on its own, achieve all the goals associated with societal well-being. However, every company, regardless of its size, can make a difference in some small, yet meaningful way, in the communities in which they operate, and more and more attention is being focused on the impact that companies have within their communities. Focusing on the community level allows an organization to set meaningful targets and implement programs that fit the scale of its operations and which can provide the most immediate value to the organization and its stakeholders. Societal well-being projects and initiatives must ensure that the organization does not compromise, and instead improves, the well-being of local communities through its value chain and in society-at-large. This book is a comprehensive guide to community engagement and investment, beginning with a survey of community-related voluntary standards and then turning to strategy and management, community engagement, community investment, and reporting and communications on community-related activities.

Keywords

community; engagement; community investment; community development; corporate philanthropy; CSR

Contents

CHAPTER 1

Introduction

Sustainability is about the long-term well-being of society, an issue that encompasses a wide range of aspirational targets including the sustainable development goals (SDGs) of the 2030 Agenda for Sustainable Development adopted by world leaders that went into effect on January 1, 2016. The SDGs, which include, among other things, ending poverty and hunger, ensuring healthy lives and promoting well-being for all, ensuring inclusive and equitable quality education and promoting life-long learning opportunities for all, are based on the recognition that society in general is vulnerable to a number of significant environmental and social risks including failure of climate-change mitigation and adaptation, major biodiversity loss and ecosystem collapse, human-made environmental planning and disasters (e.g., oil spills), failure of urban planning, food crises, rapid and massive spread of infectious diseases, and profound social instability. Clearly the challenges described above are daunting and for most businesses it may be difficult for them to see how they can play a meaningful role in address them. While it is common for "society" to be identified as an organizational stakeholder, the reality is that one company cannot, acting on its own, achieve all the goals associated with societal well-being. However, every company, regardless of its size, can make a difference in some small, yet meaningful way, in the communities in which they operate, and more and more attention is being focused on the impact that companies have within their communities. Focusing on the community level allows an organization to set meaningful targets and implement programs that fit the scale of its operations and which can provide the most immediate value to the organization and its stakeholders.

While businesses generally benefit their communities by improving the standard of living and providing community members with products and services that fulfill their needs, companies can also contribute to society through philanthropy and corporate social responsibility (CSR).

Philanthropy can take many forms and includes donations of cash, products, and employee time (i.e., volunteering) to charities and other nonprofit groups. Some companies enjoy engaging in cause-related marketing, which is essentially a partnership between a company and a nonprofit that calls for the business to market its products with a promise that a portion of the sales will be donated to the nonprofit. This strategy certainly benefits the nonprofit; however, the company obviously hopes that it will see a positive uptick in sales and be able to add to its customer base. CSR initiatives vis-à-vis the community includes recruiting and training disabled veterans and providing flexible schedules and benefits to Olympic athletes to support their training activities.

While the potential benefits of community engagement and investment for businesses are often framed as being readily apparent, it is useful to consider ideas about the specific aims and objectives of corporate community involvement. One comprehensive list included making people inside and outside the community aware of various problems in the community; ensuring that investment and development efforts occur across all sectors of the community and in multiple areas including education, health, recreation, and employment; motivating members of the community to participate in community welfare programs; providing equal opportunities within the community for access to education, health, and other facilities necessary for better well-being; building confidence among community members to help themselves and others; generating new ideas and changing patterns of life within the community in positive ways that do not negatively interfere with traditions and culture; bringing social reforms into the community; promoting social justice; developing effective methods to solve community programs including better communications between community members and local governments; and creating interest in community welfare among community members and mobilizing those members to participate in the collective work for community development.[1]

The importance of organizational attention to its communities is illustrated by the inclusion of community involvement and development among the core subjects (along with organizational governance, human

[1] http://studylecturenotes.com/social-sciences/sociology/339-aims-and-objectives-of-community-development

rights, labor practices, the environment, fair operating practices, and consumer issues) mentioned in ISO 26000: Guidance on Social Responsibility first issued by the International Organization for Standardization in 2010.[2] In the overview of the subject included in ISO 26000, the need for organizations to focus on community involvement and development was explained as follows:

> It is widely accepted today that organizations have a relationship with the communities in which they operate. This relationship should be based on community involvement so as to contribute to community development. Community involvement—either individually or through associations seeking to enhance the public good—helps to strengthen civil society. Organizations that engage in a respectful manner with the community and its institutions reflect and reinforce democratic and civic values.[3]

Community engagement and investment activities provide organizations with important opportunities to leverage the impact of their contributions given that businesses typically rely on their local communities as a source of talent for the employee base, for contractors for services that the organization seeks to outsource and, of course, as a market for the organization's products and services. By contributing to educational and health programs in the community, an organization can increase the skills base of potential workers, thereby reducing training costs when new employees are hired, and lower the risk of adverse impacts to productivity due to illnesses among its employees or their immediate family members, either of which can cause employees to miss time at work. Organizations can provide financial support, as well as licensed technology, to launch a local network of engineers, scientists, and/or software developers to generate innovations that not only benefits the organization but also provided new opportunities for other members of the community, thus improving overall community well-being. Finally, the proximity of local customers makes it easier for an organization

---

[2] International Organization for Standardization, ISO 26000. 2010. *Guidance on Social Responsibility*, Geneva.

[3] Id. at 60.

to develop and communicate their marketing messages and seek and obtain feedback on the effectiveness of those messages and the quality and value of the product and services distributed by the organization. In fact, one of the compelling reasons for investing in community involvement at all levels is the relative ease of collecting and analyzing information relating to operational performance. Proximity to the human, technical, and other resources that can be developed and nurtured through community involvement and development also allows organizations to move more quickly to seize opportunities and obtain a competitive advantage.

Community engagement must be a permanent part of the strategy and operations of any organization and this means identifying community stakeholders as soon as possible and moving quickly establishing communications and understanding their needs and expectations regarding the organization and how it will operate within the community. Organizations need to under the issues that concern community members; the beliefs, values, and experiences that drive the actions of community members and how community groups interact with one another. Organizations also need to carefully select that best strategies for their relationships with their communities, typically choosing from among community investment, which is essentially a one-way process of providing information and resources to the community (e.g., information sessions, charitable donations, employee volunteering, etc.); community involvement, which involves two-way communications, such as consultation processes prior to launching a major project; and/or community integration, which involves sharing information and consultation in advance of launching collaborative projects that are jointly controlled with, and often led by, community groups.[4]

Community Development

Community engagement and investment by organizations is part of the larger wave of CSR. Ismail noted that the classical view of CSR had actually

---

[4] Network for Business Sustainability. September 14, 2012. "Engage Your Community Stakeholders: An Introductory Guide." https://nbs.net/p/engage-your-community-stakeholders-an-introductory-gui-615902ab-e363-47ff-a3fc-d87188938739

been limited to corporate philanthropy; however, the focus has gradually shifted toward emphasizing the relationship between business and society and contributions that companies can and should make to address social problems.[5] The result of this evolution has been the current concept of CSR in which business organizations consider the interests of society by taking responsibility for the impact of their activities on customers, suppliers, employees, shareholders, communities, and other stakeholders as well as their environment. This means not only complying with applicable laws and regulations, but also acting in an ethical manner and proactively and voluntarily taking steps to improve the well-being of their employees and their families and the communities in which they are operating.[6]

One of the most-cited aspirations for business organizations with respect to their communities is providing a positive impact on community development and improving the quality of life and levels of well-being among the members of the community.[7] One description of community development provided by Ismail referred to the process of developing active and sustainable communities based on social justice and mutual respect through initiatives undertaken by a community with partnership with external organizations or corporations to empower individuals and groups of people by providing those groups with the skills (i.e., how to make use of local resources and build political power through the formation of large social groups working for a common agenda) they need to effect change in their own communities.[8] Another interesting, and admittedly broad, definition of community development includes "intentional collective actions to improve social, economic, physical, and environmental well-being, while preserving valuable aspects of the culture of

---

[5] Ismail, M. Fall 2009. "Corporate Social Responsibility and Its Roles in Community Development: An International Perspective." *The Journal of International Social Research* 2, no. 9, p. 199.

[6] Id.

[7] International Organization for Standardization. Geneva, 2010. ISO 26000: Guidance on Social Responsibility, 61.

[8] Ismail, M. Fall 2009. "Corporate Social Responsibility and Its Roles in Community Development: An International Perspective." *The Journal of International Social Research* 2, no. 9, pp. 199–203.

the particular geographic area."[9] Priorities with respect to well-being vary depending on the area and the level of economic and social development therein. For example, in the developed countries in North America and Europe community development tends to focus on housing issues; however, in less developed countries the concerns of community members tend to be coping with and overcoming threats to stability and fending off war, disease, famine, extreme poverty, and environmental dangers.

In 1971 the United Nations described community development as an organized effort of individuals in a community conducted in such a way to help solve community problems with a minimum help from external organizations such as government and nongovernment organizations and business enterprises of various types and sizes.[10] This definition emphasizes creativity and self-reliance among community members while providing opportunities and duties for external organizations and businesses to contribute through CSR practices that provide education and organizational skills to the community.[11] Self-reliance is also an important element of the related concept of "community work," which Ismael described as being about "the active involvement of people in the issues that affect their lives and focuses on the relation between individuals and groups and the institutions which shape their everyday experience."[12] In the context of community work, businesses have a role in enabling sharing of skills, awareness, knowledge, and experience in order to bring about change in the community.

Common Roles of CSR in Community Development

Surveys have shown that commitment to CSR and related activities is an important driver of employee engagement and that employees care a great

---

[9] https://useful-community-development.org/definition-of-community-development.html

[10] United Nations. 1971. "Popular Participation in Development: Emerging Trends in Community Development." New York, NY UN Department of Economic Affairs.

[11] Ismail, M. Fall 2009. "Corporate Social Responsibility and Its Roles in Community Development: An International Perspective." *The Journal of International Social Research* 2, no. 9, pp. 199–204.

[12] Id.

deal about how their employer is perceived with respect to social responsibility in the communities in which they operate. CSR is a multifaceted concept that involves relationships with multiple stakeholders including investors, employees, customers, and suppliers as well as with the local communities in which companies operate and society as a whole; however, it is possible and useful to review the following list of some of the common roles of CSR in community development prepared by Ismael:[13]

- Business can share in the negative consequences resulting from industrialization, as is the case when companies operating higher emission vehicles pay a higher road tax in order to reduce the tax burden on small vehicle owners in the community and allow community members to re-channel their funds to more productive uses within the community. Business often invest in infrastructure to facilitate easier access to their facilities for deliveries and outward-bound shipments and doing so in a socially responsible fashion means being mindful of the impact of such activities on traffic patterns of local residents.
- CSR activities focused on the local community build closer ties between businesses and their communities, support a peaceful coexistence, and build social capital that is essential to community development. This explains why community engagement to collect information and forge relationships is such an important part of every community development effort undertaken by companies.
- Organizations with a reputation for CSR can take advantage of their status and strengthen their appeal as an attractive employer by making their commitment part of their value proposition for potential candidates. In addition, when employees have a favorable opinion of the CSR of their employers they score better on various measures of performance and have more confidence in senior management.

---

[13] Id. at 205–206.

Happy and motivated employees are better ambassadors of the company in the community.

- Closer ties between businesses and their communities promote better transfers of technology into the community in several ways including the flow of human resources; the flow of private support for the research and development efforts in the public sector (e.g., corporate underwriting of technology development at local public universities); and the flow of technology from the business directly into the local community in the form of more affordable and higher quality products and services.

- CSR helps to protect the environment in communities through the efforts of businesses to reduce their own environmental footprint and provide financial, managerial, and technical support to local nonprofits involved in initiatives focusing on the protection of the environment. Activities that harm the local environment are clearly visible to community members and thus make it difficult to create the positive relationship mentioned above. In turn, protecting and honoring the local environment by supporting the creation of parks sends a powerful message throughout the local community.

- CSR is based on a commitment by businesses to universal principles in relation to the protection of human rights and involvement in their local communities allows companies to take a proactive role in promoting social inclusion, both directly and through partnerships with other organizations. Among other things, businesses can set an example in their communities through the way that they align their operations and strategies within the areas of human rights and labor and the requirements regarding human rights they impose on local suppliers.

- A CSR program can be seen as an aid to alleviate poverty in local communities. Businesses can contribute cash and other resources directly to organizations working to improve the lives of community members living below the poverty line and can marshal the resources of other community members through cause-related marketing activities (e.g., allocating customers to earmark a portion of the purchase price for the company's products for contribution to local groups working on alleviation of poverty).

- A CSR program can help in gathering data that can be used by governmental agencies and other organizations in their own community development programs. For example, technology companies can assist understaffed police departments with information gathering and processing by installing cameras with video processing abilities in areas where there are high rates of crimes in order to improve safety and security in the local community.

Management of Community Development Activities

Successful engagement by businesses in the development of their communities requires a number of core competencies and contributions from a number of groups and departments within the organization. Businesses must have the skills and resources to understand community and community development, build capacity within the communities that they operate, establish and maintain effective communications and relations with community leaders and groups, and develop and implement strategic business and community partnerships. In addition to a central management group dedicated to community relations, which might also include a corporate community foundation, businesses will need to martial support and assistance from personnel involved in marketing, human resources, health and safety, environmental management, ethical investment, public relations, and community resource development.[14]

Ways for Businesses to Contribute to Community Development

ISO 26000 describes community development as improving the quality of life and levels of well-being among the members of the community.[15]

---

[14] Id. at 207.

[15] International Organization for Standardization, ISO 26000. 2010. *Guidance on Social Responsibility*, 61, Geneva.

Participation in community development projects are a means for organizations to directly and more effectively contribute, at the local level, to solving overriding societal development challenges that cannot be completely addressed through public policies alone and which require contributions from all organizations. In fact, certain of the overriding global commitments and goals with respect to sustainable development, such as environmental sustainability and the universal availability of fully productive, appropriately remunerated and freely chosen employment, cannot realistically be achieved without the proactive support and participation of businesses. Businesses also have the financial and human capital, as well as the technology, to supplement the often meager resources of governmental bodies in their communities in efforts to eradicate extreme poverty and hunger, improve primary education opportunities, promote gender equality and empower women, and improve health and combat disease.

Community development is not the sole responsibility of organizations operating in the community, but rather comes from community stakeholders working together out of a sense of shared responsibility. From that perspective, the goal for each organization is to find the best way for it to contribute, and the commentary included in ISO 26000 suggests that organizations can contribute by:[16]

- Creating employment through expanding and diversifying economic activities and technological development
- Making social investments in wealth and income creation through local economic development initiatives both within and outside the organization's core operational activities
- Expanding education and skills development programs
- Promoting and preserving culture and arts
- Providing and/or promoting community health services
- Facilitating and participating in institutional strengthening of the community, its groups and collective forums, cultural, social and environmental programs and local networks involving multiple institutions

---

[16] Id.

- Supporting related public policies and engaging in partnerships with governmental agencies to pursue development priorities identified during the course of the community's own deliberative processes
- Engaging with a broad range of stakeholders with special emphasis on identifying and consulting with and, where possible, supporting vulnerable, marginalized, discriminated or under-represented groups
- Engaging in socially responsible behavior

Community Development and Core Business Activities

ISO 26000 explains that some activities of an organization may be explicitly intended to contribute to community development, while others may aim at private purposes but indirectly promote general development. For example, programs focusing on preserving local culture and arts, which typically take the form of financial support and employee volunteerism, are generally unrelated to the core operational activities of the business but presumably provide value through enhancement of the reputation of the business and tighter integration with various segments of the community. On the other hand, investing in improvement to access roads and other aspects of the transportation infrastructure in the areas next to the facilities of the business not only provide direct operational benefits to the business but also are likely to provide indirect benefits to the community if the changes are well planned after consultation with impacted groups within the community. While each of the contributions listed above are important, businesses, regardless of size and like any other type of organization, do not have unlimited resources, nor do they necessarily have the expertise to make a significant impact, at least initially, in each of the areas. Every business has the capacity to continuously engage in socially responsible behavior; however, ISO 26000 notes that beyond that the most important contributions to community involvement and development will depend on the circumstances in the community itself, the unique knowledge, resources, and capacity each organization brings to the community and the degree of alignment between the activity and the core operational activities of the business.

It makes sense that the most efficient way for an organization to contribute to community development is through applying its inherent skills base and selecting and implementing projects that are closely related to its core business activities. There are many activities that businesses engage in as part of the ordinary course of their operations and ISO 26000 counsels that by explicitly integrating the concept of community development and involvement into the planning and implementation of those activities the business can minimize or avoid negative impacts and maximize the benefits of those activities and sustainable development within the community. ISO 26000 provides the following list of examples of ways in which execution of the core activities of an organization can also contribute to community development:[17]

- An enterprise selling farm equipment could provide training in farming techniques
- A company planning to build an access road could engage the community at the planning stage to identify how the road could be built to also meet the needs of the community (e.g., by providing access for local farmers)
- Trade unions could use their membership networks to disseminate information about good health practices to the community
- A water-intensive industry building a water purification plant for its own needs could also provide clean water to the community
- An environmental protection association operating in a remote area could buy the supplies needed for its activities from local commerce and producers
- A recreational club could allow use of its facilities for educational activities for illiterate adults in the community

Another sampling of how companies linked their community development activities to their business competences and resources included the following illustrations:[18]

---

[17] International Organization for Standardization, ISO 26000. 2010. *Guidance on Social Responsibility*, 63, Geneva.

[18] Highlights from IFC's Good Practice Handbook. February 2010. *Strategic Community Investment: A Quick Guide*, 8. Washington DC: International Finance Corporation.

- A bank's employee volunteer program capitalized on one of the bank's core competencies—its microfinance know-how—to deliver high-quality pro bono consulting services to microfinance institutions in emerging markets.
- A company donates space in its local factory for use as classrooms for public schools in order to support the local government's efforts to alleviate a critical shortage of classrooms.
- A technology-focused company partners with a nonprofit focused on educational issues to establish technology learning centers in communities located in remote rural areas to foster new social and economic opportunities.
- A mining company worked with local farmers to increase yields through use of fertilizers that contained by-products of the mining company's normal operational activities.
- A technology-focused company used its technology to indigenous peoples monitor destruction of the forests in which they lived.
- A charitable foundation established by a large multinational company used its resources and powers of persuasion to create a partnership among financial institutions and other investors to provide access to finance for community entrepreneurs.
- A company sent its trainers to educate its supply chain partners on awareness and prevention of infectious diseases and created programs to disseminate health information to consumers in the communities in which the partners were located.

Core business competencies can come in many different forms and may include research and development, convening power, supply chain contacts, access to consumers, business know-how, facilities, equipment, logistics, and staff time and expertise.[19]

Startups and Small Businesses

While corporate philanthropy and social investment are commonly discussed with respect to larger businesses, there are significant and effective ways for startups and smaller firms to engage with their communities

---

[19] Id.

and have a positive impact that enhances their reputation and morale of their employees. Some of the ideas that should be considered by entrepreneurs and small business owners include sponsoring the activities and/or specific events of nonprofit organizations in the community; incorporating employee volunteering into the company's mission and personnel policies; designing a business model that "gives back" to the community (e.g., setting aside a portion of the profits from each sale for automatic investment toward a solution of a community social or environmental issue); contributing to the local economy by prioritizing hiring from within the community and selecting local vendors for procurement of necessary goods and services; and promoting local businesses to customers and other contacts through co-marketing efforts or referrals.[20]

Larger organizations typically have formal business units or teams focusing on various aspects of community involvement and development ranging from philanthropy; employee volunteerism; infrastructure investments and collaborations on local issues relating to education, health, safety, and the environment. At their startups, sustainable entrepreneurs need to approach community involvement pragmatically, recognizing that how they demonstrate appreciation for the surrounding community will have a profound impact on the organizational culture that emerges from the launch phase. Sustainable entrepreneurs need to put community involvement and development high on their agendas, even as they are struggling with creating the company's initial products and services, and seek to identify not only what their communities can provide for the business but also what the business can offer to the community in exchange.

When a company is first launched, the contribution of the business may be limited to the time and experience of employees who participate in community activities with the blessing and support of the company. While seemingly modest, these interactions will hopefully provide a foundation for a positive reputation for the business in the community, which can be enhanced by making a concerted effort to conduct meetings in the community to forge relationships with community leaders and prospective employees and other business partners. Other ideas for sustainable

---

[20] Berger, B. August 24, 2016. "5 Ways Entrepreneurs Can Enhance Local Communities." *Entrepreneur*, https://entrepreneur.com/article/280501

entrepreneurs looking for easy, yet potentially impactful, ways to quickly and efficiently start getting involved with their local communities include sponsoring events and activities of community-based nonprofit organizations; incorporating volunteering into the overriding purpose and mission of the business; identifying way to incorporate "giving back" into the company's business model; contributing to the local economy by making commitments to buy supplies and raw materials from local vendors and partnering with local businesses for services and other business-related purchases; and promoting other local businesses through co-marketing efforts and/or through referrals.[21]

For many startups, the first community is an online group that includes early adopters and users of the company's product or service and others such, as representatives of the media and prospective investors, who have an interest in the progress of the company. In most cases, the primary interest of the startup in its online community is growth of that community, hopefully with accompanying revenues; however, engagement with an online community should be done with the same goals and purposes that organizations become involved with traditional communities: building relationships, enhancing reputation and social license to operate, soliciting information and ideas that can be used in the business, attracting the interest of potential investors and other strategic partners and recruiting talent. Surveys among startups regarding their approaches to online community involvement and management identify a variety of useful ideas and strategies including recruitment of an experienced "community manager" as a high priority.

Community management is not to be confused with social media management, although mastering the technical and marketing aspects of engagement through social media is important. Community managers in this context practice meaningful engagement with community members regarding the company's products and services and the specific needs and expectations within the community, crucial information in a situation where it is relatively easy and costless for users to switch to a different platform. In fact, sustainable entrepreneurs often argue that community

---

[21] Id.

management is not the right term; the proper perspective is on engagement and eliciting participation in the vision by community members. The engagement process should involve building connections within the community so that members are able to communicate with one another, rather than just with the company, and do so in a manner that is transparent and amenable to discussion of problems with the way the company is handling a particular issue. Eventually, as resources permit, companies can expand engagement beyond online channels to include live events in areas where a significant pool of community members are located. Startups can also forge strategic partnerships with other organizations to offer related products and services to community members. In the meantime, the information obtained through community management can be used to focus the startup's efforts on the one or two things that really need to be done next in order for the company to scale efficiently.[22]

---

[22] For additional ideas and case studies relating to startup strategies relating to community management, see Barba, R. May 15, 2015. "Startups Share Their Tactics and Thoughts on Community Management." https://tech.co/startups-share-tactics-thoughts-community-management-2015-05

CHAPTER 2

Strategy and Management

Community engagement and investment is a multifaceted activity that requires formal management and planning. Working with and in the community is part of the broader corporate social responsibility (CSR) activities of the company and this means that management should begin at the top of the hierarchy with the board of directors or, in most cases, the committee of the board that has been delegated responsibility for overseeing CSR activities on behalf of all of the directors. The CSR committee, working in collaboration with senior management of the company and specialists working specifically on community-related matters, should be tasked with developing strategies and policies relating to community engagement and investment; deciding on the optimal organizational structure for community-related activities, including perhaps the formation of an affiliated corporate foundation; ensure that procedures are in place for conducting due diligence on prospective recipients of grants and other resources from the company and potential partners in community development projects; development and approval of projects; overseeing implementation of projects, including preparation of definitive agreements with community partners, monitoring progress, and measuring impact; and compiling and analyzing relevant information regarding community activities for presentation in the company's sustainability reporting.

Strategy Development

The first step in the process of designing, implementing, and managing the company's community engagement and investment should be developing appropriate strategies and policies. If the company's activities are limited to occasional actions that fall into the realm of traditional philanthropy (i.e., small grants to local nonprofits and/or annual volunteering days), it may actually be that it has no specific strategy, which may be fine for a short period of time when the company is just launching and has scarce planning resources that need to be focused on other issues. However, as companies take on more ambitious plans with respect to involvement with communities and tackle issues that cannot be solved with one act, such as addressing poor education and poverty in the community, long-term strategies that go out three to five years are appropriate since the company's resources will need to be committed to the issue over an extended period of time. Strategies should describe what the company expects to achieve over the planning period in relation to its vision, mission, and goals with respect to community development and how it plans to achieve those goals in terms of organizing and committing its available resources.

The development of a strategy is the time for the CSR committee, and the company as a whole, to focus on three fundamental questions. First, the company should decide on the group within their community that will be the primary target of the activities. For example, many companies prefer to be involved in programs for young people in their communities, such as improving primary education and/or providing recreational spaces. Other groups that might be targeted include older people, community members with disabilities, and groups that have been marginalized and/or discriminated against due to gender or ethnicity. The next thing that needs to be done is to determine whether activities should be focused on specific parts of the community, such as a particular neighborhood, or can and should be scaled to have an impact throughout the entire geographic area. For most companies, the answer, at least initially, should be to concentrate on the areas surrounding the company's facilities. Finally, in order to have a strategy the company needs to decide on the sector and related issues on which the community-related activities will concentrate. Sector refers to the broader community development area, such as education, health, the environment, job creation, and/or some of the other topics discussed below. Issues are specific aspects of the selected sector, such as early childhood education in the education sector, encouraging regular medical screenings and tests in the health sector and entrepreneurship training in the job creation sector. Decisions regarding sector and related issues should be made with an eye toward how the company, with its specific resources and competencies, can make the greatest impact in alignment with its overall vision and mission.

As is the case generally when the task is strategic planning for a business, the CSR committee and others involved in the planning process need to review the past and current community-related activities of the company to assess whether they are in alignment with the vision, mission, and goals that the company wishes to incorporate into its new strategy. A study should be done of the practices and activities of comparable organizations and, most importantly, the plan should not be developed and implemented without extensive community engagement in order to understand the priorities and expectations among community members and anticipate how the community might react to a particular initiative or program. When selecting the target groups, sectors, and issues, reference should be made to technical guidance and standards that have been developed for community engagement. Developing the strategic plan will initially be a time-consuming process; however, once the plan is in place, it should be easier to review and modify to take into account changing circumstances. Companies should expect to assess and update their plans no less frequently than annually during the planning period and wholesale revision of plans will usually be required every four to five years.

Setting Objectives

In order for businesses to be able to develop and implement a strategic plan with respect to their community engagement and investment activities and design their organizational structures in a way that will align with that plan, they must develop a vision of the world they would like to see, identify their specific mission in achieving that vision, and develop objectives and targets that can be used as guides for their decisions and actions in furtherance of their vision and mission.[1] In the context of contributing to community development, companies might begin with a *vision* of a

---

[1] Community Toolbox: Developing a Strategic Plan and Organizational Structure—Developing a Strategic Plan—Creating Objectives, https://ctb.ku. edu/en/table-of-contents/structure/strategic-planning/create-objectives/main

world in the not so distant future in which community members can live without fear of contracting a particular disease or other debilitating health condition. To promote achievement of the vision the company will identify and commit to a specific *mission* that is aligned with its unique skills and resources. For example, a mission aligned with the above-described vision might be working to ensure that community members have access to the highest quality medical care and that supporting appropriate community wide initiatives for activities that, done well, are likely to push the community toward the state described in the vision. The next step is setting *objectives* and the strategies required to achieve them. Objectives must be specific and measurable and are often constructed by reference to *how much* of *what* will be accomplished by *when*. Several objectives will be attached to a particular mission, such as working to provide a certain minimum percentage of the local population (how much) with easy and affordable access to screening and treatment (what) by a date that is five years down the road (when).[2]

Individuals intuitively understand the importance of objectives in their day-to-day lives. For example, a person may have a vision of a nice meal at a restaurant on the other side of town and commit to a mission of traveling from his or her current location to the restaurant to arrive at the appointed time for the meal. The objectives associated with this activity include planning for the various aspects of the journey to the restaurant, which calls for taking into account other activities earlier in the day, availability of transport, traffic conditions, and the like. Organizations have similar reasons for explicitly focusing on objectives for each of their organizational missions. One useful summary of good reasons for organizations to develop specific objectives included the following:[3]

- Developing objectives helps organizations create *specific* and *feasible* ways in which to carry out their mission

---

[2] Id.

[3] Community Toolbox: Developing a Strategic Plan and Organizational Structure—Developing a Strategic Plan—Creating Objectives, https://ctb.ku.edu/en/table-of-contents/structure/strategic-planning/create-objectives/main

- Completed objectives can serve as milestones and indicators to demonstrate to stakeholders of the organization, including the community as a whole, the impact that the organization's actions have had on the community
- The process of creating objectives helps organizations set priorities for its goals and properly allocate scarce resources
- It helps individuals and work groups set guidelines and develop the task list of things that need to be done (and also allows for creation of scorecards that can be used to measure individual and group performance against the tasks that need to be completed in order to achieve the objectives)
- It reemphasizes the organization's mission throughout the process of change, which helps keep members of the organization working toward the same long-term goals
- Developing the list of objectives serves as a completeness check, to make sure the organization is attacking the issues associated with the mission on all appropriate fronts, and as an opportunity for internal and external engagement

In order to develop objectives, it is useful to understand the various types of objectives and the characteristics of the best objectives. It has been suggested that objectives can be broken out into three basic types: behavioral, community-level outcome, and process objectives. Each of these can be illustrated by reference to a neighborhood home improvement group. Behavioral objectives focus on changing behaviors of community members (i.e., what they are doing and saying) and the results of their behaviors. With respect to home improvements, the changed behaviors might be an increase in home repair activity with the result that the quality of housing in the community improves. Community-level outcomes are the aggregate of individual behavior changes, in this case an increase in the percentage of people in the community who live in adequate housing. Finally, processes are the foundation for achieving the other objectives and an appropriate process objective for the neighborhood group might be adopting a comprehensive plan to improve housing in the neighborhood community.[4] Any type of objective should be checked to see how it conforms to the following characteristics:

- It should be *specific*, which means that it should identify *how much* (e.g., 20 percent) of *what* is to be achieved (e.g., what behavior of whom or what outcome) *by when* (e.g., by a specific date).
- It should be *measurable*, which means that it is reasonably feasible that information concerning the objective can be collected, detected, or obtained from records (and plans for measurement should be prepared in advance of starting the project).
- It should be *achievable*, which means the objective not only reasonable and possible but that it is likely that the organization can, through its efforts, be successful.
- It should be clear how pursuit and achievement of the objective is *relevant* to the organization's overall vision and mission.
- It should be *timed*, which means there is a timeline developed by the organization by which the objective will be achieved.
- It is *challenging*, which means that although the objective is achievable (as noted above), it will not be easy and can be expected to stretch the group in order to achieve significant improvements that are important to members of the community.[5]

While thoughtful and well-done objectives make perfect sense when they are presented, the process of creating objectives is not easy and organizations should expect to invest a significant amount of time and effort on the process and proceed methodically through several important steps. The first thing to do is to reconsider the organization's vision and mission statements, which means stepping back and looking at the "big picture" about what the organization wants to achieve with regard to its programs of participation in and contributions to its community. The goal is to identify gaps between the situation in the community at the current moment and the organization's vision of how things should be in the community by an identifiable date in the future. Identification of gaps allows the organization

---

[4] Id.

[5] Id.

to begin creating a list of the changes that will need to be made in the community in order for the organization's vision to be realized. Organizations should seek input from a number of sources when they begin inventorying potential changes including experts in the specific field or topic, specialists within the organization, change leaders in the community, and, of course, the potential targets and beneficiaries of change. As ideas come in, the organization needs to begin considering resource and logistical challenges associated with participating in a particular change effort (e.g., additional funding, new staff, and/or training for existing staff, members).

The goal of this whole process is to compile a list of the changes that would need to be made in order to move closer to the organization's vision for the community and which are reasonably within the scope of the organization's own mission (i.e., the specific contribution that the organization feels it can make to achievement of the vision). From that list, the organization can develop a sensible set of objectives for its community development activities that are aligned with its current resources and feedback from the community as to what should be prioritized. One reference for organizations on developing their objectives posited an illustration based on the assumption that the organizational mission statement was "reduction of risk for cardiovascular diseases through a community-wide initiative" and that the organization had compiled a fairly lengthy list of general goals from which objectives could be crafted:[6] Begin smoking cessation programs

- Begin smoking prevention programs
- Bring about an increase in aerobic exercise
- Decrease the amount of obesity
- Encourage healthier diets
- Increase preventative medicine (e.g., more checkups for earlier detection of disease; better understanding of warning signs and symptoms)
- Increase the organization's scientific understanding regarding the causes and pathophysiology of cardiovascular disease

---

[6] Id.

- Strengthen the organization's ties with national organizations committed to the same goals as the organization

Few would argue that all of the goals listed above are worthwhile; however, each goal brings its own set of issues, challenges, and resource requirements and the next step is to set priorities and align progress on each of the goals in a systematic manner. All this begin with collecting baseline information on each of the goals, which means compiling and analyzing data that allows the organization to get an accurate picture of the scope of the issue or problem in the community. Organizations should collect data on the incidence of a problem in the community (i.e., new cases, such as how many community members reached a level of health that would be defined as obese in the last year), the prevalence of a problem in the community (i.e., existing cases, such as what percentage of the community would be classified as obese), and attitudes relating to a problem in the community (i.e., what percentage of the community thinks there is a problem and that it is important to address). Baseline data can be used to demonstrate create the case for taking action and as the foundation for measuring success if work on a particular goal is eventually incorporated into the organization's community development objectives. Baseline data can be collected from publicly available sources, such as government publications; other organizations that are involved in similar issues and which are willing to share their data; and from surveys, questionnaires, and interviews within the community itself. Community-sourced data is extremely valuable and its availability will obviously depend on the organization's ability and willingness to engage effectively with community groups and individual community members.

The baseline data provides the organization with an idea of the scope of the problem or issue and a better idea of the specific elements that should be included in the objectives in the event that the organization decides to take the problem or issue on. At this point the organization needs to assess its resources and determine if they are sufficient to provide the organization with a reasonable opportunity to achieve its objectives. Decisions are difficult to make since it is impossible to predict the impact of the organization's efforts with certainty, particularly if substantial collaboration from other groups will be required on the community project or initiative. Given all this, this is the point in the process where the organization needs to prepare its initial list of objectives, which should address anticipated behavioral changes, community impacts and the planning process, include a timetable for attainment and fit each of the characteristics described above. Before the objectives are finally approved for implementation within the organization, they should be reviewed one last time by the key internal and external stakeholders to ensure they address the expectations of everyone who will be involved in the project or initiative. This is also the time to check to be sure that the objectives are sufficiently complete to address the problem or issue and evaluate how the objective will be perceived by stakeholders (e.g., taking on a controversial health issue may alienate certain groups in the community at the same time it attracts the support of other groups). Another thing to consider is how progress on each of the objectives will eventually be reported to the organization's stakeholders. Once the objectives have been settled on the organization can turn to development of strategies for achieving each of them.

Obviously it is important to develop objectives before launching any community-related project or activity; however, setting, verifying, and, if necessary, changing or abandoning objectives is a continuous process that is essential to the vitality and sustainability of any organization's community involvement and development efforts. Checking objectives should occur whenever the organization is involved in reviewing its overall vision and accompanying missing statements. Objectives should also be revisited in connection with any decision to change or expand the focus of the organization's community development efforts. For example, a change or expansion may become feasible if and when the organization gains access to additional financial resources or new technologies. Finally, objectives are necessary for projects that cannot be completed quickly (i.e., projects that will take several years to complete and measure, such as increasing the percentage of students in the community that finish high school, or projects intended to change behaviors in large numbers of community members, such as increasing the level of physical activity in the community) and/or which require a multifaced approach (e.g., a project focused on reducing substance abuse—reducing the prevalence of drug use (how often or how much)—needs to address several issues simultaneously such as restricting access to drugs, making drug rehabilitation services readily available in the community, and policymaking related to the legal consequences of drug use).[7]

Organizational Structure

Another part of the strategic planning process, generally addressed in most detail once decisions have been made regarding sector, issues, and objectives, is deciding on the best organizational structure for implementing and managing the plan as well as the extent to which reliance will be placed on the resources and skills of outside parties. Companies generally have several options to choose from and may use more than one approach as part of a comprehensive community engagement and development program. In some cases a project or event may be executed through an internal group or department, such as sponsoring a community picnic. Companies often establish a separate legal entity, such as a corporate foundation, to manage community-related activities. Use of a separate nonprofit entity allows the company to leverage their own resources with funding from other sources (i.e., government programs and grants from other foundations) and to create a separate and distinct organizational structure for community activities with job titles and responsibilities that are aligned with the activities that need to be executed in the community area. Regardless of whether a company creates an internal group or a separate entity, job descriptions, and roles and responsibilities need to be prepared and defined for all team members and appropriate connections need to be forged between the community engagement and development team and departments and groups within the company that can provide support such as budgeting, procurement, accounting, finance, administration, and information technology.

Using an internal group or a controlled foundation are both examples of companies retaining substantial control over the implementation and management of a project; however, it is often necessary, and easier, for companies to make grants to an outside party better qualified to implement a particular project (or enter into a partnership or alliance with an outside party that provides for the outside party to take on a substantial amount of the work associated with the project). Several factors need

---

[7] Id.

to be considered when deciding between executing a project through an internal group and/or controlled foundation and outsourcing execution:

- Outsourcing may be easiest when the company can readily identify a competent and experienced local party that is already focused on the specific sector and issue and has projects in place that are aligned with the company's vision and goals.
- Retaining control is preferred when the company needs to have the flexibility to customize the program to fit its specific vision and goals.
- When cost is a significant factor, use of an outside party often makes the most sense since they already have invested in the resources and skills necessary for effective implementation—if the company takes the project on it will generally not be able to achieve and enjoy the advantages of "economies of scale" since it will need to purchase/lease the necessary tangible and intangible assets and hire and train additional human resources.
- Control is obviously a key distinction between the two approaches, with companies seeking high levels of control over the project opting to execute on its own (in some cases, it is possible to negotiate control over an outsourced project through governance provisions in the agreements with the outside party; however, those may be of limited value unless the company actually places its own personnel into the project).
- The type of project and long-term goals and projected activities of the company with respect to the sector and issue are relevant and outsourcing may be preferred for relatively straightforward projects where the outside party can provide effective project management while executing a project internally is the best course of action when the company's specific project management know how is needed and the project is part of the company's efforts to gain deeper knowledge of the sector and issue that can be used in subsequent projects.

Decisions regarding the optimal organizational structure depend on the portfolio of community engagement and investment activities that the company has selected in the process of developing its strategies for that area. At any given point in time, a company may be engaged in a wide array of programs and initiatives including employee volunteering, direct corporate contributions (i.e., non-foundation), foundation giving, matching gifts, federated campaigns, cause marketing, social innovation, workplace giving, social enterprise, partnerships, etc.[8] The issue, as discussed elsewhere in this chapter, is ensuring that the portfolio is optimally designed to achieve the greatest business and community impact and decisions regarding portfolio design will lead to changes in the organizational structure.

Evaluating Outside Partners

When it appears that the best path of action for the company is to rely on an outside party to perform a significant amount of work associated with a prospective project, the company (either the internal group or the controlled foundation) must follow an orderly process, referred to as "due diligence," to determine the risks and benefits of working with a particular outside party. For that matter, due diligence of the type described below should be performed whenever a company makes a direct grant and/or contribution of other resources to a local nonprofit organization. Due diligence should be undertaken after the parties have had preliminary discussions to confirm a mutual interest in some sort of collaboration, the terms of which will eventually be laid out in formal documents.

A good deal has been written about due diligence process, which typically includes review of publicly available documents and reports and documents provided on a confidential basis by the outside party, site visits, and interviews with representatives of the outside party and their clients from previous projects. While information will come from various sources, the idea is to get answers with respect to several key issues and questions relating to the outside party:

- The identity and history of the outside party: The legal identity and status of the outside party; the period of time that it had been in existence and providing the services that it

---

[8] Rochlin, S. 2017. *The Business ROI of Social Investments*, IO Sustainability.

currently performs; affiliations of the party with organizations and governmental bodies relevant to the proposed project; permits and licenses; public image; and any ongoing litigation or regulatory disputes

- The skills and resources of the outside party: Measures of the competence of the outside party (e.g., capacity, expertise, and years of experience) with the geographic areas, sectors, and issues to be covered by the proposed project

- The governance and management of the outside party: Information regarding the composition of the board of directors of the outside party including profiles of board members and advisors; diversity in expertise; frequency and scope of board meetings; overall vision, mission, and strategy of the outside party; relevant experience of the management team and specialists that would be involved in the particular project; and actual and potential conflicts of interest

- The operational processes of the outside party: Organizational structure and deployment of human and physical resources; operations, systems, and processes; human resources and risk management

- The financial capability of the outside party: Availability and review of financial statements and reports of financial condition required to be made with regulatory bodies with oversight responsibility in order to determine adequacy of reserves and efficiency of prior management of capital and additional audit of internal controls

- The level of transparency regarding operations practiced by the outside party: Compliance with legal disclosure requirements and additional requirements imposed due to expectations of stakeholders of the outside party (e.g., funders and members of community served by the outside party)

The end product of the due diligence process should be a due diligence report that meets the criteria established in advance for evaluating the outside party for the specific project. The report should cover all of the issues and questions listed above as well as the compatibility of the outside party with the company's own vision, mission, and goals with respect to community engagement and development. As the company gains experience in the due diligence process, more formal procedures can be established and the company will have more experience and context that can be used to assess the results of the due diligence process on any one outside party. If the outside party is selected, provision should be made in the formal agreements with the outside party for continuous updates of information with respect to the outside party in many of the areas described above including financial statements, reports, and material changes in activities.

Once the due diligence investigation of the outside party has been completed (or the due diligence investigation of a potential grantee has been completed when the company is making a grant on its own, either directly or through its corporate foundation), attention turns to completing and approving a project proposal. Responsibility for developing the project proposal lies with the party that will be actually implementing the project on behalf of the company (i.e., the internal group, the corporate foundation, or the outside party) and should be based on information regarding the geographic, sectorial, and issue-based targets for the project collected from governmental and other sources and, most importantly, stakeholders in the community that will be impacted by the project. A good project proposal should cover the overall context for the project in the community including the current and projected roles of other stakeholder engaged with community development; the key needs of and issues confronting the target beneficiaries of the project; project goals, key performance indicators, baselines, and expected end results; milestones to be used for purposes monitoring the progress and performance of the project; budgets; risk management, and mitigation strategies; and details regarding reporting of progress and impact of the project.

Project Development

Project development is crucial to the success of the project and calls for attention to a range of different, albeit related, activities:

- Developing a framework to identify and engage with key stakeholder groups in the local community including local governmental bodies, research institutions and universities, prospective funders for the project, and the intended beneficiaries of the project

- Conducting an assessment, if required, to identify and evaluate developmental needs and priorities in the community, a process that requires a number of different tools at various levels of participation (e.g., interviews, community meetings, surveys, etc.)
- Studying and adopting best practices to address similar challenges based on prior experiences or lessons available from other organizations and communities
- Clearly describing the proposed project including the objectives of the project; the intended beneficiaries and the anticipated impact on those beneficiaries; key assumptions; the expected outputs and outcomes; and a detailed list and description of activities
- Identifying the key performance and success indicators for the project and the means for measurement and verification (including measurement and verification of baselines against which the project performance can be compared)
- Creating a reasonable budget for the project that includes all feasible funding sources such as governmental sources, other corporate donors and/or contributions from community members (including community-based nonprofit organizations)
- Selecting and implementing the methods that will provide a clear measure of the impact of the project on the company, the community, and other involved parties

One of the objectives of developing the project proposal is to provide decision makers with sufficient information to review and approve the project. Approval should be based on finding that the proposed project aligns with the goals and objectives that have been established for community engagement and development, the proposal incorporates indicators for monitoring project progress and measuring impact and that sufficient resources have been allocated to the project. The amount of time required for the review and approval of a proposal will depend on various factors including the size and scope of the project and the company's prior experience with similar projects and/or the outside party selected to assist with implementing the project. The project proposal should be accompanied by a due diligence report. The decision makers, which may be the members of the CSR committee of the board of directors or the board of directors of the corporate foundation that the company has set up to manage community development activities, may suggest or require changes to the proposal as a condition for approval and any such changes should be incorporated into the final version of the proposal.

In some cases, the final approval of a project to be implementing with an outside party will not occur unless and until a memorandum of understanding or other form of definitive agreement has been agreed upon with the outside party, which agreement would be part of the proposal package submitted to the decision makers. Such an agreement should define the roles, responsibilities, deliverables, and commitments for each of the parties and the consequences in the event either of the parties breaches their obligations under the agreement. Each agreement should describe the expected outputs and impacts based on objective measurement criteria established at the beginning of the project and the outside party should commit to collecting the data necessary for proper measurement. Agreements should also cover the processes for communication between the parties, dispute or conflict resolution mechanisms, inspection and audit requirements, timelines and milestones, and, of course, the procedures for disbursing funding to the outside party based on a budget agreed upon in advance that includes reasonable conditions regarding continued progress of the project. In situations where the amount of resources being committed to a project is not large and/or the company has prior experience with the outside party, approval of a project may be given without a final form of definitive agreement and authorized representatives of the company will be delegated the authority to negotiate and execute an agreement on their own provided that it conforms to the company's standard practices.

Monitoring and Reporting

Once the project has been approved and the definitive agreement has been completed, it is time to focus on monitoring the progress of the project to ensure that everything is on track and to collect information about the process, the sector and the issues that can immediately be incorporated into the development of new projects. Proper monitoring requires timely information and may also be facilitated by the use of independent auditors. Interactions with the intended beneficiaries of the project are important at this phase as they obviously can provide essential input as to whether or not the project as then designed is meeting their needs and expectations with regard to the target issue. A number of tools and methodologies have been developed for measuring impact and companies need to understand how they will be deployed with respect to a particular project and set aside the resources to create meaningful impact reports. Impact measurement often requires a dedicated team that can visit the site where the project is being conducted and conduct interviews and distribute surveys among the target group. If the intended impact is not being achieved, changes can be made to the manner in which the project is being implemented.

Once the project is completed (or at least annually in the case of projects that are expected to run over multiple years), a project report should be completed for presentation to the decision makers and, in many cases, for publication to the stakeholders of the company impacted by the project and the company's overall community engagement and development activities. As mentioned above, the project proposal and definitive agreement should include procedures for collecting the information necessary for preparation of reports and the company should decide in advance on the reporting framework it will follow in order to ensure that the information necessary to comply with the framework is available. When preparing the report, due regarding should be given to the expectation of the intended recipients including the members of the CSR committee, investors, and other parties providing funding for the specific project, government agencies, and members of the community. As the company's community-related projects scale up, a reporting specialist will generally be recruited to ensure that reporting practices are consistently applied.

Selecting the Sector and Related Issues

As noted above, one of the fundamental questions that must be addressed at the very beginning of the development of a strategy for community engagement and investment is the selection of the sector(s) and related issues on which the company's community-related activities will concentrate. A sector is a broader community development area, such as those described below, and issues are specific problems or challenges within a sector upon which a company's strategy, resources, and competencies can be properly and effectively focused. In many cases sectors will be selected on the basis of the personal priorities of the founders and other organizational leaders of the company and/or the core business activities of the company. While relying on these inputs is helpful, companies should be careful not to settle upon sectors and issues without first conducting an assessment of the needs within the community and the expectations of community members regarding the company's involvement and investment. For example, the activities and geographic location of a company may dictate that prioritization be given to a specific sector, such as engagement with and support for indigenous peoples.

Companies can look to a variety of sources to assist them in compiling a list of sectors and related issues from which choices can be made including the ISO 26000 Guidance on Social Responsibility developed by the International Organization for Standardization,[9] the Future-Fit Business Framework, the OECD Guidelines for Multinational Enterprises (http://mneguidelines.oecd.org/), the STAR Community Rating System framework (STAR),[10] and the United Nations Sustainable Development Goals

---

[9] International Organization for Standardization, ISO 26000: Guidance on Social Responsibility (Geneva 2010).

[10] The STAR Community Rating System (STAR) (www.starcommunities.org) was launched in 2008 as a framework and certification program for local governmental and community leaders to assist them in assessing the level of sustainability in their communities. The STAR framework is based on a holistic set of Guiding Principles with respect to local sustainability that include thinking— and acting—systematically; instilling resiliency; fostering innovation; redefining progress to include not just GDP but also improvements in the health and well-being of the community's people, environment, and economy; living within means; cultivating collaboration; ensuring equity; embracing diversity; inspiring leadership and continuously improving. STAR Communities has officially merged with the U.S. Green Building Council. Together and the two groups are in the process of developing a new, expanded LEED ("Leadership in Energy and Environmental Design") for Cities & Communities program that incorporates the best of the STAR Community Rating System within the LEED rating system structure.

(SDGs) of the 2030 Agenda for Sustainable Development.[11] For those companies interested in participating in addressing one or more of the SDGs at the community level, reference can be made to the resources available through SDG Funders (www.sdgfunders.org) in order to gain a better understanding of how businesses, nonprofits, and other types of organizations have been supporting initiatives focused on one or more of the SDGs. Among other things, the SDG Indicator Wizard is a simple and innovative tool that organizations to identify which of the SDGs are most closely aligned with its existing strategic priorities as declared in organizational mission statements and then use that information to create an SDG-compatible framework that includes relevant goals, targets, and indicators. Additional guidance for businesses on creating strategies that will allow them to contribute to progress on the SDGs is provided by the SDG Compass (www.sdgcompass.org) and addresses defining priorities, setting goals, integration and reporting, and communications.

Building the Business Case

While many hope that community engagement and investment initiatives will be compelling in their own right because of the need for businesses to participating in addressing significant challenges, needs, and threats in their local communities, the reality is that executives and managers proposing community projects must be prepared to demonstrate a strong business case for those initiatives in order to mobilize sustained commitment to them throughout the organization and ensure that the appropriate resources are allocated to the initiative and that the necessary changes are made to company's measurement, management, recognition, and reward systems.[12] As evidence for the importance of the business case, Willard, who has written extensively on best practices among companies

---

[11] http://un.org/sustainabledevelopment/sustainable-development-goals/

[12] Willard, B. 2017. "Introduction." In *Sustainability ROI Workbook: Building Compelling Business Cases for Sustainability Initiatives* (May 2017 Edition) (the Workbook, which is regularly updated, is available for download, along with other information on corporate sustainability projects, at http://sustainability-advantage.com/).

with respect to sustainability, pointed to a report by Bain & Company, "Achieving Breakthrough Results in Sustainability," that was based on a survey of over 300 large companies engaged in sustainability efforts and found that 98 percent of their sustainability initiatives had failed.[13] According to Bain & Company, one of the five reasons for this dismal failure rate was "lack of a compelling business case."

While the results of its survey were discouraging, Bain & Company believed that companies could improve their performance with respect to sustainability initiatives by following four guidelines: "make a public commitment," "lead by example at the top," "highlight the business case," and "hardwire change through incentives and processes." Willard argued that a compelling business case should be seen as the prerequisite for the other three guidelines since executives could not reasonably be expected to do any of the other things unless they were convinced that the initiative was good for the company and its direct stakeholders (i.e., investors, employees, and customers), as well as good for the environment and for society as a whole. Willard also pointed out that "strong leadership support," cited by Bain & Company as one of five factors that contributed to successful sustainability initiatives, could only be expected if the business case was strong enough to earn the endorsement, engagement, and proactive support of company executives and senior managers and that such support paved the way for the other success factors mentioned by Bain & Company: "employee engagement and interest," "clear goals and metrics," "effective internal communication," and "introduction of environmentally friendly policies/processes." Willard made his pragmatic case for focusing on the business case for sustainability initiatives as follows:

> We need to meet executives where they are and honor their need for compelling ROI information when they assess proposals. If an initiative improves the company's reputation, grows revenue, saves expenses, engages employees, helps win the war for talent, spurs innovation, meets company norms for payback periods, provides a good internal return on investment, increases the value

---

[13] Id. Citing and describing Davis-Pecdoud, J., P. Stone and C. Tovey. January 2017. *Achieving Breakthrough Results in Sustainability*. Bain & Company.

of company assets, and/or contributes to higher share prices, of course executives will support it.[14]

There are a number of different methods that can be used to develop a business case; however, Willard has developed a customized approach that he recommends for sustainability executives and managers looking to build the business case for sustainability initiatives. Willard's "sustainability return on investment" workbook "provides a comprehensive cost-benefit analysis framework by which to build a tailored business case for single or multiple sustainability initiatives implemented within various timeframes," is extensively annotated and should be consulted directly for practical guidance on developing and implementing sustainability initiatives.[15] The elements of Willard's method for developing the business case for a sustainability project or initiative are based on his assumption that there are only three reasons that companies undertake major projects and that these justifications for investment must be borne in mind when making the case for implementation to decision makers:

- "Do the Right Thing": This justification means activating the company's purpose and values, being ethical, and making sure that projects and initiatives are aligned with the company's strategic direction and mission. Willard explained that something is "right" when it improves the well-being of stakeholders and that since society and the environment are stakeholders there is a strong justification for sustainability projects and initiatives that improve their well-being by reducing harmful impacts and increasing positive impacts. In addition, a sustainability project or initiative may be the "right thing" for the decision maker's own personal values, well-being, and aspirations.
- "Capture Opportunities": This crucial justification speaks the need to the chief executive and financial officers to accommodate the needs of the company's investor

---

[14] Id.
[15] Id.

stakeholders by not approving any sustainability project or initiative that cannot be cost justified over a specified planning period, be it short or long term. When presenting a business case consideration must be given to the specific financial metrics that are motivating the decision makers and these may vary and can include return on investment, reductions in expenses, top-line revenue growth, and/or the impact of the project or initiative on the company's investment market value and share price.

- "Mitigate Risks": Willard explained this justification as being the flip side of "Capture Opportunities" and pointed out that prudent stewardship of the company's assets and principles of good governance demanded implementation of robust enterprise risk management processes. Part of those processes is examining each new project or initiative from a risk management perspective and that requires that business cases must quantify risks that could arise if the project or initiative was not undertaken and the risks that could arise if the project or initiative fails.

While each of the justifications should be addressed in every business case the appropriate weighting will depend on the particular circumstances and the personal concerns and approaches of the decision makers involved. In many cases, capturing opportunities and/or mitigating risks will remain the predominant factors for decision makers, even as the company is looking to integrate sustainability into its operations; however, the need to "do the right thing" is becoming increasing important as non-investor stakeholders, such as employees and customers, apply pressure on executives to take societal and environmental well-being into account. Moreover, when a company decides to "do the right thing" by improving working conditions for its employees, it will hopefully see that the company's capacity to capture opportunities will be enhanced due to the involvement of a happier and better trained workforce.

Willard argued that each business case for a sustainability project or initiative should include several common elements, each of which is related to one of the justifications described above:

- When a project or initiative is recommended as being in furtherance of the desire to "do the right thing," it must be aligned with the company's purpose, values, mission, vision, principles, beliefs, and long-term strategic goals.
- When a project or initiative is recommended as a means for capturing opportunities, it should include a cost-benefit analysis and return on investment assessment that supports one or more particular categories of opportunities such as revenue growth from improved company reputation with customers, innovative sustainable products, services, and financing and strong brand and social license to operate; operational expense savings and improved efficiencies or human resource expense savings (e.g., lower hiring and attrition costs and increased productivity). Additional opportunities may be available with respect to asset and/or market value improvement.
- When a project or initiative is recommended as a means for mitigating risks, the business case should address mitigation of risks of inaction (i.e., if the initiative is not undertaken by the company and its competitors do) and mitigation of risks of taking action (i.e., if there might be cost overruns, delays, or collateral damage). For example, a project or initiative may be appropriate to mitigate the risk of lost revenue from poor company reputation with customers; the risk of lost revenue from outdated products and services; or the risk of higher energy, carbon, materials, water, waste, maintenance, travel, and/or transportation expenses.

The business case should also address potential benefits to the company with respect to "reputation" and "innovation"; however, it should be acknowledged that impact and value to these areas from a particular project or initiative will be difficult to quantify in the same manner as revenues and expenses. In spite of the measurement challenges, successful projects and initiatives can improve reputation with customers, which may drive revenue growth; improve reputation with employees that drives engagement and productivity that eventually leads to human resources expenses savings; and improve reputation with investors that causes the company's market value to increase. In addition, projects and initiatives that produce new revenues and cost savings are generally new and innovative and will lead to advances in many operational areas including policies, products, processes, and practices.

Structuring Corporate Philanthropy Initiatives

While there are a number of different ways that for-profit businesses can "give back" to their communities by making gifts of cash and other items to charities and other nonprofit organizations, it is important to understand three basic methods that are commonly used for philanthropic activities: direct-giving programs; a company foundation formed and sponsored by the business, which can be a private foundation or a public charity; and a donor-advised fund. Businesses are not limited to just one of these methods and may shift the focus of their philanthropic activities from one method to another as time goes by and the goals of the philanthropic program change. For example, smaller businesses will generally begin with a modest direct-giving program in order to conserve resources. As the business expands and revenues sufficient to support more ambitious philanthropy become available, it may be appropriate to establish a foundation while continuing direct giving for certain types of causes and programs.[16] Regardless of whether a company creates an internal group or a separate entity, job descriptions and roles and responsibilities need to be prepared and defined for all team members and appropriate connections need to be forged between the community engagement and development team and departments and groups within the company that can provide support such as budgeting, procurement, accounting, finance, administration, and information technology.

Direct Giving

A direct-giving program is the simplest method for engaging in corporate philanthropy. One or more charities or other nonprofit organizations in

---

[16] The discussion in this section is adapted from various sources including Petit, S. 2010. *A Basic Guide to Corporate Philanthropy*. Adler & Colvin.

the community are selected for support, often with input from employees and members of the local community, and the business contributes cash or other items of value (i.e., products) that the donee can use to fulfill its own mission within the community. In many cases, provision will be made for employee matching gifts so that the entire effort builds connections between employees and the company. There is no need to create a separate legal entity to engage in direct giving and such programs are not subject to public disclosure requirements or the complex rules described below, which are applicable to company-sponsored foundations. If the company wants to be able to deduct its contribution it should ensure that the donee is tax-exempt under Section 501(c)(3) of the Internal Revenue Code (IRC) and organized in the United States. This is important because giving to a nonprofit entity is not sufficient to assure deductibility if the entity is not also eligible under the IRC to receive charitable donations. Special rules apply regarding the amount of charitable contributions that can be deducted each year and how contributed property will be valued for purposes of determining the deductible amount. Charitable contributions can either be "unrestricted," which means that the donee can decide how they are used, or made subject to specific instructions from the donor that they be used for a particular charitable purpose. Records should be created and maintained to substantiate that contributions were made and how the value of donated property was determined.

Businesses can, and often do, launch and design direct-giving programs that are highly structured and managed by a separate group within the organization, often with input from employees who are allowed to make recommendations on grants and volunteer programs and from community leaders serving as outside advisors. In many cases, however, direct-giving activities are conducted in an ad hoc fashion with no specific budget or strategic purpose. For example, companies may be approached by community groups to purchase tables at fund-raising dinners or donate products that can be raffled off to raise funds for a local school or community arts facility. Indirect contributions may be made by paying employees for the time they spend volunteering for local charities. All of this is worthwhile and creates goodwill among employees and within the communities in which the business is operating. It also allows companies to get started with their philanthropic programs without significant administrative costs. Increasingly though businesses have realized that philanthropy can and should be viewed in a strategic fashion in order to provide better value to both donors and donees and bring more efficiency to the philanthropic process. In order to achieve these benefits, consideration should be given to creating corporate foundations to plan, execute, track, and publicize significant philanthropic initiatives.

Corporate Foundation

Simply stated, a corporate foundation is a separate legal entity formed by and closely affiliated with the company, which is to be organized and operated in a manner that reflects the mission and interests of the company and its stakeholders. While corporate foundations generally rely primarily, if not exclusively, on regular contributions from the company to support their giving activities it is also possible for the foundation to solicit funding from public sources in order to expand the potential range of the foundation's work. Like any business, a corporate foundation decides each year how much of its assets will be currently deployed in philanthropic activities and how much will be set aside as an endowment reserved for future use. Establishing a corporate foundation provides the company with flexibility to make its philanthropic contributions in a way that is most efficient from both a tax and overall financial perspective. For example, if the company is having a profitable year it can make a larger tax-deductible contribution to the foundation, thus reducing the company's tax bill while enhancing the resources of the foundation without straining the financial assets of the company. The contributions made during profitable years will be available in later years to support continuity in the foundation's programs even if the company itself is not doing as well in those years and thus is not able to make a current year contribution to the foundation. Using a corporate foundation allows companies to impose stronger requirements on donees regarding the use of grant funds and also allows company executives to direct requests for support of charitable causes to an external unit that is still aligned with the company's strategy and mission but has its own decision-making procedures. However, to avail itself of the advantages of a foundation, particularly the potential tax benefits, companies need to be prepared to understand

and adhere to the complex laws and regulations applicable to private foundations or public charities and make public disclosures regarding the management and activities of the foundation.

Corporate foundations are nonprofit organizations and the predominant form of nonprofit organization is the corporation. There are several distinctions between nonprofit and profit corporations: a business corporation generally exists to make a profit for its shareholders; however, a nonprofit corporation (particularly a charitable organization) exists primarily to advance a purpose or objective; a business corporation ultimately benefits the shareholder or shareholders, but nonprofit corporations generally do not have shareholders and are not even required to have a class of members that the organization serves (however, in many cases a corporate foundation will be organized as a nonprofit corporation with a single member, the company that is sponsoring the foundation, so that the sponsor can exert influence over the corporation's activities); the goal and focus of the management of charitable organizations should be to advance the entity's stated purposes, rather than the interests of any group of individuals affiliated with the charity; and although nonprofit organizations need revenues to sustain their operations, much of these revenues will be in the form of contributions or grants (i.e., contributions from the company in the case of a corporate foundation); the pursuit of enterprises or activities solely to generate a profit can jeopardize an organization's tax-exempt status.

Donor-Advised Fund

Companies wanting to add more formality to their corporate philanthropy beyond direct giving but which are not yet ready to form a new legal entity as a corporate foundation can create a separate fund (although not a separate legal entity) that is held within an existing public charity, such as a local community foundation or the charitable affiliate of a financial services provider. The company would contribute funds or assets to the public charity that would be allocated to a "donor-advised fund" maintained by the public charity, so named because the company or its designee (e.g., the CEO of the company) would retain the right to provide advice or recommendations to the public charity on how grants should be made from the fund and how unused funds should be invested. The donor-advised fund is usually named after the company (e.g., "The [name of company] Fund" or "The [name of company] Foundation") and the public charity, as the charitable owner and sponsoring organization of the fund, deducts a small percentage of the fund assets or received contributions as compensation for its services.

Donor-advised funds are a relatively simple and inexpensive way for companies to obtain the reputation advantages of a philanthropic foundation and provide companies with the same sort of flexibility from a cash flow and tax deductibility perspective as setting up a corporate foundation as a separate entity (i.e., if the company is having a profitable year it can make a larger tax-deductible contribution to the donor-advised fund, thus reducing the company's current tax bill, and those contributions can be retained in the fund and used in later years to support continuity in the foundation's programs even if the company itself does not have sufficient funds to done to the donor-advised fund in those years). However, the funds are legally a gift to the sponsoring organization and once made are subject to the sponsoring organization's right to make final decisions regarding use of the funds (i.e., the company's opinions are only advisory, although as a practical matter the sponsoring organization will generally act in a manner that is consistent with the company's preferences provided that the mission of the sponsoring organization has been properly vetted before the fund was established). In addition, the funds will be subject to all of the internal policies and procedures of the sponsoring organization and IRS rules prohibiting benefits to donors from grants made from a donor-advised fund. Another factor to consider is that use of a donor-advised fund, even if the fund is named after the foundation, may not provide the company with as much recognition with the ultimate beneficiary, although this may be addressed to some degree by messaging that notifies beneficiaries that the grant they see as coming to them from the charity was "made possible" by the company.

While donor-advised funds have traditionally been thought of as investment vehicles for companies since they were first authorized in the early 1990s, recently they have frequently been used by individuals who have become wealthy as a result of public offerings of shares of the companies that they founded and who decide to create their own donor-advised funds by contributing securities immediately following the offering when the valuations, and resulting tax deduction, are stunningly high. For example, donor-advised funds have been launched by the founders and/ or senior executives of Facebook, Netflix, Twitter, Google, WhatsApp, and Microsoft. While these launches often were done with great publicity, the actual impact of these commitments has been questioned by some since donor-advised funds do not have to report on their activities in the same way as corporate foundations. There is evidence that large grants are being made through these donor-advised funds (e.g., donations by Facebook founder Mark Zuckerberg through his donor-advised fund to hospitals and schools in the San Francisco Bay Area); however, skeptics have pointed to other situations where stock was contributed at a high valuation but subsequently declined in value, thus reducing the amounts available to charities while allowing the donor to retain the highest tax benefit (another criticism is that the distributions from donor-advised funds can be deferred indefinitely at the discretion of the donor).[17]

Legal Considerations

The legal issues associated with the community engagement and investment activities of an organization will depend on the decisions made by the organization regarding the types of contributions that will be made (i.e., cash, in-kind, human resources, etc.), the nature of the projects and activities that will be supported and the specific topical areas of interest. As discussed above, all businesses will need to determine the appropriate legal and organizational structures for their community-focused activities and this often means that a decision will eventually need to be made about whether to form a separate legal entity, owned and controlled by the parent company, through which community investments will be funneled (i.e., a corporate foundation). Other common legal issues arise due to the nature of the business' involvement in the community and would include mitigating potential legal risks associated with employee volunteer programs, sponsoring and/or hosting community events, and

---

[17] For further discussion, see Gelles, D. 2018. "A Trendy Philanthropic Loophole." *New York Times* (August 5, 2018), B1.

entering into joint ventures and other types of alliance arrangements with local nonprofit organizations. Specialized legal guidance will be required when businesses get involved in complex and high-regulated areas such as helping to provide financial services for low-wealth and underserved communities, supporting public and private financing of community cultural facilities, participating in community-based efforts to preserve open space while expanding the availability of affordable housing and assisting local courts looking to positively and proactively address juvenile delinquency by providing vocational training and job opportunities.

Measurement and Assessment

Whenever a business is involved in a strategic planning exercise, provision must be made for regular and continuous measurement and assessment of performance against the goals and objectives that should have been established early in the planning process. Measurement and assessment of a company's performance with respect to community engagement and investment is not only important to the company, but also to the employees for which community engagement is a valuable motivator, the communities in which the company operates and, of course, the investors that provide a significant amount of the funding that ultimately is transformed into the resources that the company distributes in its community investment programs. Effective community investment also matters to customers and other business partners. Measurement and assessment is also an opportunity for further engagement with community groups and other stakeholders in that part of the assessment process should involve sitting down with partners to discuss how projects have gone and, hopefully, build further trust during those discussions. Measurement and assessment of community engagement and investment should be conducted as part of the company's broader practice of "social auditing," which has been described as a comprehensive evaluation of the way a company discharges all its responsibilities to shareholders, customers, employees, community, and the government. A simple four-step process for conducting a social audit would begin with an itemization of all the activities of the company that have a potential social impact and then continue with an explanation of the circumstances leading to these actions or activities, an evaluation of the performance and impact of each of the actions or activities and an examination of the relationship between the goals of the company and those of society to see how each of the actions or activities related to one another.[18] Social audits have two main purposes: an internal evaluation of a company's social responsibility performance and a means for collecting and organizing the information required in order to make public disclosures of a company's social responsibility performance.

The impact of social actions and activities on economic performance is certainly relevant; however, the primary focus of the social audit should be on gaining a better understanding of the company's contributions to and participation in activities that promote the well-being of employees and community members and protect the environment. Categories of information to be collected, evaluated, and eventually incorporated into both internal and external reporting on social responsibility should include community involvement (i.e., socially oriented activities that are primarily of benefit to the general public); human resources (i.e., activities directed to the well-being of the employees); physical resources and environmental contribution (i.e., activities directed toward alleviating or preventing environmental deterioration, such as pollution, and actions taken to comply with applicable environmental laws and exceed legal standards in areas such as air quality, water quality, etc.); and product or service contribution (i.e., the impact of company's product or service on society including product quality, packaging, advertising, warranty provisions, and product safety). When designing the social audit process, consideration should be given to the needs of internal stakeholders looking to incorporate the information in the audit into their decision-making processes; however, the design process should also anticipate reporting to key external stakeholders such as financial institutions, stockholders, academic institutions and consultants, governmental bodies, trade unions, political leaders, environmental and social activists, and community leaders.[19]

---

[18] Social Responsibilities of Business toward Community, https://account learning.com/social-responsibilities-business-towards-community/

[19] Social Audit/Definition/Objectives/Need/Disclosure of Information, https:// accountlearning.com/social-audit-definition-objectives-need-disclosure-of-information/

Measurement and assessment of community engagement and investment is also related to reporting on such activities. Companies that following the reporting framework of the Global Reporting Initiative (GRI) (www.globalreporting.org) will need to be able to describe their managerial approach to the indirect economic impacts of their operations including a discussion of the work undertaken by the organization to understand indirect economic impacts at the national, regional, or local level and an explanation of whether the organization conducted a community needs assessment to determine the need for infrastructure and other services (and, assuming such an assessment was done, a description of the results of the assessment).[20] Specific disclosures required under the GRI framework should address community investments, engagement with local communities and actual and potential negative impacts of the organization's actions on local communities. The reporting framework proposed by the London Benchmarking Group focuses on helping companies better quantify and organize information about their corporate community investment activities and, most importantly, assess and report on the impact of their relationships with communities and how to manage it.[21] Another idea for measuring and assessing community engagement and investment was provided by Willard, who suggested that assessing whether an organization had achieved "fitness" with regard to soliciting and addressing community concerns could be expressed as the proportion of communities potentially impacted by business operations who have ready access to well-functioning concerns mechanisms capable of addressing any issues quickly, fairly, and transparently.[22]

---

[20] GRI 203: Indirect Economic Impacts 2016. 2016. Amsterdam: Global Sustainability Standards Board.

[21] Reporting on Community Impacts: A Survey Conducted by the Global Reporting Initiative, The University of Hong Kong and CSR Asia (Amsterdam: Stichting Global Reporting Initiative, 2008), 6.

[22] Willard, B. May 2017. "Society Wellbeing." In *Sustainability ROI Workbook: Building Compelling Business Cases for Sustainability Initiatives* (Edition) (the Workbook, which is regularly updated, is available for download, along with other information on corporate sustainability projects, at http://sustainability-advantage.com/).

CHAPTER 3

Community Engagement

Communities generally appreciate most of the tangible benefits that companies provide including jobs, support for local businesses and non-profit organizations, and assistance with maintaining the infrastructure upon which all community members depend. However, there is at least one other important thing that companies can do to improve the quality of life in their communities and make better use of their own resources. The answer is proactively working to give community members a "voice" by allowing them to have input into decisions made by governments, companies, and other organizations that will impact their day-to-day lives and the level of well-being in the communities in which they live and work. Community engagement is the cornerstone of everything a company does vis-à-vis the community in which operates.

Community engagement appears in many of the voluntary standards relating to sustainability and reporting on sustainability-related matters. For example, the OECD Guidelines for Multinational Enterprises (http://mneguidelines.oecd.org/) call on enterprises to seek and consider the views of community members before making decisions regarding changes in operations that would have major effects on the livelihood of employees and their family members living in the community and the community as a whole (e.g., proposed closures of facilities) and take steps to mitigate adverse effects of such decisions on the community. The Global Reporting Initiative (GRI), (www.globalreporting.org), created Sustainability Reporting Standards that have become the most widely used standards on sustainability reporting and disclosure around the world and which call for reporting organizations to discuss their management approach to local communities by describing the means by which stakeholders are identified and engaged with; which vulnerable groups have been identified; any collective or individual rights that have been identified that are of particular concern for the community in question; how it engages with stakeholder groups that are particular to the community (for example, groups defined by age, indigenous background, ethnicity, or migration status); and the means by which its departments and other bodies address risks and impacts, or support independent third parties to engage with stakeholders and address risks and impacts.[1]

In its *CSR Processes and Practice Manual*, Africa Oil Kenya (AOK) noted that a company's approach to working with local communities is a critical component to its social license to operate and cultivating a trusted relationship, with strong communication, between the company and its community stakeholders takes time and patience.[2] Among other things, community engagement should be used to proactively understand the various perspectives of the communities in order to manage the expectations of stakeholders, identify potential conflicts or risks and appropriate responses, and ensure communities feel like they have been engaged. Effective stakeholder engagement requires a deliberative and ongoing process based on the following principles and elements:[3]

- *Predictability*: Stakeholders should have a clear understanding of the process of engagement
- *Transparency*: Information should be communicated early in the decision-making process in ways that are meaningful and accessible
- *Accessibility and Appropriateness*: Consultation with stakeholders should be conducted in a manner that is inclusive and adapted for local norms in order to ensure that stakeholders can communicate effectively and with minimal barriers (e.g., financial, cultural, literacy restraints, etc.)
- *Responsiveness*: Engagement should help the company understand and respond effectively to issues as they emerge.

---

[1] GRI 413: Local Communities 2016 (Amsterdam: Global Sustainability Standards Board, 2016).
[2] *Corporate Social Responsibility Processes and Practices Manual: Operating Guidelines* (Africa Oil Kenya B.V., July 2015).
[3] Id.

- *Documentation*: Engagements to be documented for future reference in order to ensure that the company can respond appropriately and to support transparency of engagement
- *Grievance Mechanisms*: Grievance mechanisms should be incorporated into the engagement process in order to allow for open communication of issues from stakeholders and enable company to proactively manage critical issues.

One striking feature of the construct of community involvement and development is the emphasis on proactive engagement by businesses and other organizations with the individuals and groups within the communities that the organization operates, either as a resident of the community (e.g., the area in which the organization maintains its principal offices), as a vendor of products that are commonly used within a community or as a consumer of natural resources that are available in the community. Businesses should not simply make their own judgments and decisions about what is best for the communities in which they operate but instead should take the time, and invest the resources, necessary to establish a framework for continuous engagement with the communities in order to better assess the needs and expectations of the community and select and launch projects and initiatives that will have the greatest positive impact on community and generate reputational advantages for the organization.

Identification and engagement of stakeholders in the community regarding the impact of the organization's activities is certainly a fundamental part of community involvement and development; however, ISO 26000 stresses that organizations must act with sincerity and demonstrate that they value their communities and that they recognize their role as stakeholders in the community with shared common interests. In other words, an organization needs to consider itself as being part of, and not separate from, the community in which it operates as it develops its approach to community involvement and development. As described by ECOLOGIA, "every business is a stakeholder in its community; it depends on the community and also affects its development."[4]

---

[4] *Handbook for Implementers of ISO 26000, Version Two* (Middlebury, VT: Ecologia, 2011), 32.

The importance of authenticity cannot be understated and organizational representatives, from the directors and members of the executive team at the top-down to the lowest levels of the organizational hierarchy, need to be mindful of how they interact with the community in both formal and informal settings. A chance encounter between a mid-level manager wearing a jacket with the company's logo and a community member in a restaurant can be just as impactful as a presentation by the CEO to the town council.

Businesses, especially larger firms, are used to dictating the terms of engagement with their commercial partners and stakeholders; however, effective community engagement by organizations means acknowledging and accepting the influence of the unique historical, cultural, religious, social, political, and economic characteristics of the community and overcoming the challenges created by differing and conflicting interests among the other stakeholders in the community. ISO 26000 emphasizes that organizational social responsibility with respect to community involvement and development means recognizing and having due regard for the rights of community members to make decisions in relation to their community and thereby pursue, in the manner they choose, ways of maximizing their resources and opportunities. Organizations must also appreciate that the value of their contributions will be enhanced by working in partnership, and sharing resources, efforts, and experiences, with other community stakeholders.

Definitions and Descriptions of Community Engagement

Community engagement does not lack for definitions and interpretations. For example, according to the Queensland government in Australia, the term "community engagement" typically refers to the process of involving people from a specified community in the development and implementation of decisions that affect them. Communities can include people who identify with a defined geographical area ("communities of place") and/or people who share a particular experience, interest, or characteristic ("communities of interests," such as young people, older people, people with a common religious or cultural background, or people with disabilities).[5] The Center for Disease Control and Prevention described community engagement as:

> … the process of working collaboratively with and through groups of people affiliated by geographic proximity, special interest, or similar situations to address issues affecting the well-being of those people. It is a powerful vehicle for bringing about environmental and behavioral changes that will improve the health of the community and its members. It often involves partnerships and coalitions that help mobilize resources and influence systems, change relationships among partners, and serve as catalysts for changing policies, programs, and practices.[6]

Community engagement is sometimes referred to as "participation" or "involvement." ISO 26000 described "community involvement" as being "an organization's proactive outreach to the community" and noted that organizations should seek involvement with their communities as a means for familiarizing themselves with community needs and priorities so that the organization's development plans are compatible with those of the community and society; preventing and solving problems; fostering partnerships with local organizations and stakeholders; and aspiring to be a good organizational citizen of the community.[7] Community involvement includes participation and support for civil institutions and interaction with networks of groups and individuals that constitute civil society. However, while involvement and engagement are important, it is not sufficient in terms of satisfying requirements and expectations of organizations with respect to environmental and social responsibility and

---

[5] *Community Engagement Toolkit for Planning* (The State of Queensland Australia: Department of Infrastructure, Local Government and Planning, August 2017), 7.

[6] *Principles of Community Engagement*, 2nd edition (Center for Disease Control and Prevention, June 2011). 3, http://www.atsdr.cdc.gov/communityengagement/pdf/PCE_Report_508_FINAL.pdf

[7] International Organization for Standardization, ISO 26000: Guidance on Social Responsibility (Geneva, 2010), 63.

organizations remain ultimately responsible for the environmental and social impacts of their actions.

As organizations look to figure out the best way to get involved in their communities they need to be mindful that there are many different types of groups, both formal and informal, that can contribute to development and which should be considered by organizations as they formulate their plans for activities in the community. ISO 26000 pointed out that one of the most common methods for community involvement is participation in forums established by local authorities and residents' associations or by creating such forums. These forums providing a comfortable level of formality that aligns with many of the skills and experiences of organizational members involved in the community development process. However, organizations cannot ignore the influence of informal groups such as traditional or indigenous communities, neighborhood associations, or Internet networks and these groups create special challenges in terms of access and being sensitive to their unique cultural, social, and political rights.

The related actions and expectations of organizations with respect to community involvement mentioned in ISO 26000 include:[8]

- Consulting representative community groups in determining priorities for social investment and community development activities, with special attention being given to vulnerable, discriminated, marginalized, unrepresented, and underrepresented groups to involve them in a way that helps to expand their options and respect their rights
- Consulting and accommodating communities, including indigenous people, on the terms and conditions of development that affect them, with consultation occurring prior to development to ensure that any organizational actions are based on complete, accurate, and accessible information
- Participating in local associations as possible and appropriate, with the objective of contributing to the public good and the development goals of communities

---

[8] Id. at 64.

- Maintaining transparent relationships with local government officials and political representatives, free from bribery or improper influence
- Encouraging and supporting people to be volunteers for community service
- Upholding the rule of law and contributing to policy formulation and the establishment, implementation, monitoring, and evaluation of development program in a manner that respects the rights and has due regard for the views of others to express and defend their own interests.

Core Principles of Community Engagement

The State of Queensland Australia, in its comprehensive guide for governmental entities on public participation and community engagement for planning and implementation of development projects, provided a set of core principles of community engagement that can be adopted for use by all types of public and private organizations:[9]

- *Engagement focuses on the best interests of the community*: Engagement should be undertaken in the best interests of the *whole* community, rather than of any individual person or group.
- *Engagement is open, honest, and meaningful*: Engagement should draw the attention of the community to all relevant information, the purpose and general effect of the proposed plan/changes, and the specific details, and the community should be provided with genuine opportunities to participate in/contribute to the plan-making process and should be kept informed of the proposed plan/changes and its implications and any amendments during the process.
- *Approaches to engagement are inclusive and appropriate*: Engagement must be inclusive, appropriate to the needs

---

[9] The State of Queensland Australia: Department of Infrastructure, *Community Engagement Toolkit for Planning*. Local Government and Planning, August 2017, 9–10.

of the community, and commensurate with the scale and complexity of the proposed plan/changes. The organization should reach out to and encourage the community to be involved in discussing planning and development issues that affect their lives, making sure to seek out diverse voices and perspectives. The organization should identify and address potential barriers to community input, while being open with the community about any budget constraints, and should make every effort to implement a mix of qualitative and quantitative engagement methods that reach the greatest number of community members, gather a diversity of opinions, and make it easy for community members with specific needs to participate (e.g. language, people with disabilities, older people, and the young).

- *Information is timely and relevant*: The organization should ensure that the community is provided with information in a timely manner that allows sufficient time for the community to consider information and make a meaningful contribution to the planning and assessment process for a program or initiative before decisions are made. Organizations need to launch engagement early in the planning process and set aside sufficient time to listen to community members and address their concerns. Organizations also need to be prepared to be flexible and change course in response to the dynamics of the engagement process.

- *Information is accurate, easy to understand, and accessible*: Community members should be confident that they will have easy access to information that is accurate, easy to read, and easy to understand; tailored to the community, where necessary, in language and style; and in a form that appeals to the intended audience. The organization needs to provide community members with clear instructions about how submissions from the community should be made and community members should understand how their submissions will be reviewed and used and the general timeframe before decisions will be made by the organization.

- *Decision making is transparent*: The engagement process should be undertaken with the stated objective of making decisions in a manner that is open and transparent. The organization should be prepared to provide community stakeholders with reasons for the decisions made by the organization and discuss with individual submitters how their submissions were taken into account.

IAP2 Core Values for Public Participation

The International Association for Public Participation (IAP2) (https://www.iap2.org/) is an international association of members who seek to promote and improve the practice of public participation/public engagement in relation to individuals, governments, institutions, and other entities that affect the public interest in nations throughout the world. The IAP2, with broad international input, developed a set of core values for the practice of public participation that cross national, cultural, and religious boundaries and which organizations can reference in developing their own community engagement processes in order to make better decisions that reflect the interests and concerns of potentially affected people and entities:[10]

- Public participation is based on the belief that those who are affected by a decision have a right to be involved in the decision-making process.
- Public participation includes the promise that the public's contribution will influence the decision.
- Public participation promotes sustainable decisions by recognizing and communicating the needs and interests of all participants, including decision makers.
- Public participation seeks out and facilitates the involvement of those potentially affected by or interested in a decision.

---

[10] https://iap2.org/page/corevalues

- Public participation seeks input from participants in designing how they participate.
- Public participation provides participants with the information they need to participate in a meaningful way.
- Public participation communicates to participants how their input affected the decision.

Ethical Conduct of Participants in the Engagement Process

Effective community engagement must be built on a sense of trust between the company and the members of the community and engagement should be carried out in a manner that conforms to recognized standards of professionalism and ethical conduct. In fact, the IAP2 has developed a Code of Ethics for Public Participation Practitioners that is intended to serve as a guide to the duties of public participation practitioners and ensuring the integrity of the public participation process. Among the guiding principles in the Code are enhancing the public's participation in the decision-making process and assisting decision makers in being responsive to the public's concerns and suggestions; building trust and credibility for the process among all the participants; carefully considering and accurately portraying the public's role in the decision-making process; encouraging the disclosure of all information relevant to the public's understanding and evaluation of a decision; ensuring that stakeholders have fair and equal access to the public participation process and the opportunity to influence decisions; and ensuring that all commitments made to the public, including those by the decision maker, are made in good faith.[11]

Benefits from Community Engagement

While community leaders and members may not always be pleased to hear that an organization is considering a particular project or initiative, they generally will appreciate the opportunity to meet with the organization, and one another, to discuss concerns; expand their understanding, and the

---

[11] https://iap2.org/page/ethics

organization's understanding, of the relevant issues; and share experiences and ideas. When properly conducted, the community engagement process promises to provide benefits and better outcomes for both the organizations and the communities with which they are engaged. In general, community engagement allows all parties to identify the concerns, risks, opportunities, options, and potential solutions that surround a particular issue or a proposed project or initiative likely to have an impact in the community. Benefits to all involved parties from community engagement might include:[12]

- Better decisions about projects and initiatives including the quality of services and other contributions provided in the community by the organization
- A better understanding of the day-to-day experience of people in communities
- Better relationships between the community and the organization
- Community awareness and understanding about an issue
- Community buy-in and higher levels of community ownership
- Greater community support for, and more effective, implementation of the project or initiative
- An opportunity to determine what will work in reality and what will not
- A mechanism for feedback/evaluation on the organization's existing community projects or initiatives
- Improved communication pathways, such as the use and further development of community networks
- Opportunity to develop individual and community capacity and shared understanding of both issues and potential solutions
- Legitimization of decisions around controversial issues
- Mutual learning and discover of new ideas and expertise
- Reduced conflict within stakeholder groups because individuals and communities can hear and understand each other's points of view, leading to consensus

---

[12] *Community Engagement Toolkit for Planning* (The State of Queensland Australia: Department of Infrastructure, Local Government and Planning, August 2017), 7–8.

Organizations and members of the community can also use the engagement process as a catalyst for increasing awareness and understanding on both sides about sustainability issues and challenges as they relate to the community and the operational activities of the organization in the community. For example, discussions in the context of a proposal for developing a new facility, or expanding or upgrading an existing facility, should include exchanges of information and opinions regarding preservation and protection of open space and the environmental impacts of operations at the facility and the proposed development and construction work. Community members join the engagement process for a number of reasons; however, in general they do so because they have a personal interest in the project or issue and welcome the opportunity to voice their opinion and meet other members of the community that share their passions and interests. Many community members participate because they have a strong aspiration to create meaningful changes in their communities. The act of engagement on a single project is often the first step to a broader and sustainable involvement in community policies.

In addition to the above-listed benefits, community engagement can be extremely valuable to the organization in the following ways:[13]

- The organization can make better decisions when developing and implementing community programs and initiatives.
- The organization can gain a better understanding of the day-to-day experiences of people in their communities, and their appreciation of their local amenity and heritage.
- The organization can develop a foundation for better and sustainable relationships with key stakeholders in the community.
- The organization can secure "buy-in" from the community for the project or initiative and enjoy higher levels of community support as a result of community members feeling they have an ownership stake in the success of the project or initiative.
- The engagement process should create an efficient and reliable communication mechanism for obtaining feedback from the

---

[13] Id. at 8.

community regarding decisions made during the planning
and implementation phases.

- Organizational personnel involved in the engagement process
will have opportunities to share their own ideas and develop
their individual capacities and skill sets in ways that will
benefit the community project or initiative and ability to take
on other roles for the organization.

The Network for Business Sustainability (nbs.net) observed that the
benefits of community engagement to businesses can include better decision making based on the knowledge collected from the community and
understanding the community's concerns and goals; more legitimacy for
the business in the eyes of the community due to the willingness of the
business to hear community views and engage in constructive debate and
conflict resolution before decisions are made; and better access to talented
workers from the community who are more willing and eager to work
for a company that has demonstrated its commitment to being a "good
citizen" of the neighborhoods in which the workers and their families live,
shop, go to school, and otherwise go about their day-to-day activities.[14]

Critical Success Factors for Effective Community Engagement

Recommendations regarding the key factors that organizations should
consider when planning for community engagement activities include
the following: have a purpose for the engagement in mind at the outset
and be clear about what the engagement process is intended to achieve;
understand the context within which the engagement process will be
carried out, which means paying attention to the needs and character
of the community; engagement is about people and effective engagement begins with identifying the community members who should be
involved, what their needs and concerns might be, and what support or
incentives might be required in order to ensure they participate; select the
engagement tools and methods that are most appropriate for the planned

---

[14] *Engage Your Community Stakeholders: An Introductory Guide for Businesses*
(Network for Business Sustainability, 2012), 3.

level of engagement and make sure they are appropriate in the specific context; and establish the goals and overall objectives for the engagement process in advance.[15] When launching an engagement process, an organization needs to be mindful of insights from exhaustive research regarding engagement that show that there are usually persons and/or groups that tend to dominate the conversation and other groups that are continuously underrepresented and must be coaxed into the process. In other words, if the engagement is conducted through public meetings, there may be a full slate of speakers drawn from the "usual suspects" but long meetings does not necessarily mean that everyone who should be heard has participated.[16] In particular, organizations may need to consider different methods for engaging with various ethnic groups and/or groups congregated in a particular geographic area in the community. Technology, including the Internet, has created new methods for engagement; however, organizations need to be careful when deploying technological tools that they do not create barriers to participation.

Effective community engagement is a skill that must be learned and continuously practiced. While people inside the organization may have talents for communicating and being empathetic to the concerns of others, these general traits need to be supplemented by specific training on how to listen and analyze, respond, facilitate resolution of conflicts, promote productive behaviors, and promote positive behavioral changes. Resources for developing effective community engagement and managerial skills are widely available from organizations such as The Community Roundtable and organizations should be prepared to train their engagement teams before they begin their involvement with the local community.[17] Beyond training special support should be available when engagement involves

---

[15] Adapted from descriptions of the International Association for Public Participation's Framework for Participation provided in "What Is Community Engagement?" available from the Homes and Community Association at www. homesandcommunities.co.uk/community-engagement-toolkit

[16] Id.

[17] For further information on the "50 Essential Skills in Community Management" developed by The Community Roundtable see https:// communityroundtable.com/community-careers-and-compensation/50-essential-skills-in-community-management/

working with community members who may have become disillusioned due to bad experiences in the past or who have fallen victim to "consultation fatigue" after too many prior meetings, forums, and activities.[18]

Framework for Levels of Community Participation and Engagement

While community engagement is an often used phrase, the meaning in a particular situation depends on various factors and there are several different approaches that companies can take with respect to engagement on a particular project. The distinguishing factor is the amount of participation and involvement from the community. The most prominent and often cited framework for public participation and levels of community engagement has been developed by the IAP2, which identifies the following five levels of engagement, each one from top to bottom of the list below with increasing levels of participation and involvement by community stakeholders in the decisions that companies make regarding their participation in community affairs:[19]

---

[18] "What Is Community Engagement?" available from the Homes and Community Association at www.homesandcommunities.co.uk/community-engagement-toolkit

[19] Adapted from descriptions of the International Association for Public Participation's Framework for Participation provided in "What Is Community Engagement?" available from the Homes and Community Association at www.homesandcommunities.co.uk/community-engagement-toolkit and *Community Engagement Toolkit for Planning* (The State of Queensland Australia: Department of Infrastructure, Local Government and Planning, August 2017), 8. Other names for specific levels of engagement are used in different frameworks; however, the five levels described in the text provide a widely accepted reference point. For example, the Network for Business Sustainability identified three broad types of engagement: community investment, which is similar to community outreach as described in the text; community involvement, which is similar to community consultation described in the text; and community integration, which is similar to community collaboration described in the text. See *Engage Your Community Stakeholders: An Introductory Guide for Businesses* (Network for Business Sustainability, 2012), 4.

- *Community Outreach and Education*: Activities at this level are focused on providing the community with honest, balanced, and objective information to assist community members in understanding opportunities, problems, alternatives, and/or solutions. The main goal is "to inform" and information dissemination is essentially a one-way process intended as a starting point for more advanced dialogue and two-way communications. Outreach may be done using a variety of techniques such as newsletters, websites, information sessions, sustainability reports, and exhibitions. Related activities are also essentially one-way arm's length transactions such as charitable donations and support of the community volunteering activities chosen by employees themselves as opposed to selections of groups and causes by the company.

- *Community Consultation*: Community consultation, discussed in more detailed below, is classical community engagement that seeks community information and feedback on analysis, alternatives, and/or decisions to be made by the company regarding its actions in the community. Consultation is often required as a matter of law in that governmental approval of a project may be conditioned upon demonstration that the applicant has invited community participation and considered community feedback before finalizing its proposal, although the company is not obligated to make changes in response to community input. Consultation involves structured activities such as focus groups, surveys, and public meetings. Consultation occurs after, or as part of, the education process at the level above and seeks answers from the community to issues that have been identified and explained during the education process. Community consultation forges stronger connections between companies and their community stakeholders.

- *Community Involvement*: While community consultation is designed to collecting information from the community about issues and prospective projects without a firm commitment to formally take community views into account, community involvement explicitly brings the community into the process in order to ensure that their concerns are considered before decisions are made. With community involvement communication is participatory with information flowing both ways and various groups throughout the community sharing information with one another. While companies practicing community involvement are not required to make changes that are advocated by community members, they are expected to report to the community on how community feedback influenced their decisions and by providing such feedback it is hope that the viability of the project will be enhanced by a sense of increased cooperation between the company and the community. Techniques used in connection with community involvement include workshops and deliberative polling.

- *Community Collaboration*: Community collaboration involves partnering with the community in each aspect of the decision including the development of alternatives and the identi-fication of the preferred solution. When companies truly collaborate with community members they are sending a signal that they want and need help from the community in order to formulate solutions to the targeted issues and that reasonable community suggestions will be incorporation into the decisions about the design and implementation of com-munity projects. Community collaboration is participatory decision making that is based on face-to-face dialogue with community representatives and individuals and groups within the community impacted by the project. Done well, commu-nication collaboration builds a sense of partnership and trust on both sides. One example of community collaboration is the formation of a committee of community members, spon-sored by the company, which will meet with managers and specialists from the company on a regular basis to come up with a solution to a problem raised by the community, such as the adverse impact of emissions caused by the company's manufacturing process. The committee would have access to the company's emissions data and the ability, with the finan-cial support of the company, to draw outside experts into the discussion to help find better ways to measure the problem and design projects that would ultimately lead to a cleaner and less toxic manufacturing process.[20]

- *Community Empowerment*: As the descriptor makes clear, this highest level of community participation and involvement places the final decision making responsibility in the hands of the community. In order for community empowerment to be effective and viable a substantial amount of time and effort must be invested in building community capacity and highly developed local structures that can effectively partner with one another and with the company or companies that are sponsoring the project. An example of such a structure would be a community development trust.

Guide to Community Consultation

Among the five levels of community engagement mentioned above it is fair to say that community consultation is extremely common and should be considered in some form for almost any community project an organization is considering. While the results of the consultation process are not binding on the organization, it increases the likelihood that a project will be accepted and understood among community members and that the assets and resources of community stakeholders will be available for leveraging when and if the project commences. The consultation process, which also includes dissemination of information (i.e., community outreach and education), allows the organization to provide community stakeholders with a clear idea of the organization's vision for the project and the results the organization seeks to obtain from sponsoring the project. By providing the community with such information and an opportunity to comment, even if community input does not substantially change the organization's decision and strategy, it will be easier to overcome resistance and often provides the organization with new ideas that actually improve the plan for the project that the organization may have initially proposed on its own. Community consultation can be usefully broken down into

---

[20] *Engage Your Community Stakeholders: An Introductory Guide for Businesses* (Network for Business Sustainability, 2012), 4.

several steps including ensuring that the proposed project responds to the needs of the local community and that the organization understands the community context; defining the community consultation plan and choosing appropriate consultation goals and methods; recording the results of the consultation process; and providing feedback to the community on the information collected and how such information was handled by the organization during its decision-making processes.[21]

Identifying Community Needs and Understanding Community Context

Organizations need to be sure that their community projects adequately address the acknowledged needs of community members. Specifically, projects must be selected and designed to respond to the particular identity, assets, resources, and needs of the community and the only way to be sure that this occurs is by consulting with the members of the community to gain an adequate understanding of the community context and the local history, demographics, socioeconomics, culture, and languages. Consultation of provides the organization with the opportunity to overcome barriers to engagement and develop effective ways of communication. In addition, consultation to identify the most significant issues and concerns among community members can be then be used to make appropriate changes to initial project proposals so that they ultimately have the highest impact in the community.

In order to understand the community context the organization needs to learn more about the socioeconomic and demographic characteristics of the area and the social, economic, and environmental challenges or priorities in the community. It is also important to understand what is already happening in terms of improvement and development activities in the community in order to figure out where the organization's proposed activities will fit with the efforts of local government and other nonprofit organizations already operating in the community. Before investing much time in meeting directly with community members to

---

[21] A Guide to Engaging the Community in Your Project, http://artscapediy. org/Creative-Placemaking-Toolbox/Who-Are-My-Stakeholders-and-How-Do-I-Engage-Them/A-Guide-to-Engaging-the-Community-in-Your-Project.aspx

gain a better understanding of these issues, organizations should survey economic, social, and demographic data and analysis that should already be available through local government agencies and other organizations such as the chamber of commerce. Major nonprofit organizations may also be willing to share information and make members of their community development teams available for consultation on how best to develop an engagement process for a particular project.

The type of data that should be collected will vary depending upon the issues that the organization is interested in addressing with its community-related projects and initiatives. For example, when the goal is to make an impact on income inequality and an absence of job opportunities in the local community, it is important to gather measurements of education, equity, and access to social resources, health and well-being, quality of life, and social capital. A sampling of relevant data points would include unemployment rates, female labor force participation rates, median household income, relative poverty measures, and the percentage of the community population with a post-secondary degree or certificate. As the scope of the project narrows to a particular neighborhood or identifiable group within the community the information requirements can be customized and sufficient information on the current state of affairs should be collected to allow for establishment of baselines, goals, and impact metrics.

One of the main goals of collecting and analyzing the data referred to above is compiling a list of the groups within the community that should be participating in the engagement and consultation process. In any given situation it is likely that engagement should be sought with resident associations, local merchant associations, local politicians, social service agencies, grassroots organizations, and other community leaders. In addition, it is essential to seek out those community members who are likely to be impacted by the project who might not otherwise be adequately represented among the more typical and formalized groups referred to in the previous sentence. One of best ways to ensure that all relevant community stakeholders have been identified and profiled is stakeholder mapping, which begins with the creation of an initial list of stakeholders and then expands to include profiles of key stakeholders (e.g., positions, interests, alliances, potential impact on community projects, and potential impact of community project on stakeholder group) and ratings of the priority levels of stakeholders. The profile for each of the key stakeholders should include their specific concerns and identify the issues that the organization will need to address strategically during the engagement process.[22]

Developing the Community Consultation Plan

Once the targets for the consultation process have been identified, attention can turn to developing the consultation plan and the selecting the activities and tools for the consultation process. When developing the consultation plan, it is important to keep the following goals and objectives in mind:[23]

- Engage community members in the development of a strong shared vision
- Inform and educate the public about the proposed project
- Bring to life the mission, vision, and values of the project
- Engender a sense of community ownership, pride, and stewardship of the project
- Create excitement around opportunities for the community to use and participate in the project and foster a sense that the project will be an anchor of community development
- Create strong relationships between the organization and the local community
- Seek champions and an ever-expanding circle of friends and supporters for the project
- Build and maintain momentum for the project

The consultation plan should set out the actions that the organization will be taking in order to manage and effectively engage key stakeholders (e.g., inform, consult closely, involve in decisions, etc.), the planned frequency of engagement and the members of the engagement team. The consultation

---

[22] *Corporate Social Responsibility Processes and Practices Manual: Operating Guidelines* (Africa Oil Kenya B.V., July 2015).
[23] A Guide to Engaging the Community in Your Project, http://artscapediy. org/Creative-Placemaking-Toolbox/Who-Are-My-Stakeholders-and-How-Do-I-Engage-Them/A-Guide-to-Engaging-the-Community-in-Your-Project.aspx

plan, as well as the stakeholder map discussed above, should be shared throughout the organization and used as a tool to institutionalize information regarding the organization's stakeholders and make it readily available to new hires and for use in internal management meetings. The consultation plan and stakeholder map should be updated regularly, no less frequently than monthly, and should incorporate all relevant information relating to incidents that occur during the course of the engagement process.[24]

Organizations will need to rely on a range of engagement and consultation methods, each of which is designed to serve a specific purpose and elicit a particular form of engagement and feedback. For example, the most basic level of engagement, which should be undertaken as the foundation for consultation, is essentially one-way communications to *inform and educate* the community about the project and related community issues. In general, these communications should be designed to share the vision, values, and goals that inform the design of the project and the organization's future operations in the community, keeping the community up-to-date on the process and progress of the project's development and providing information to community members regarding opportunities for further consultation and participation. Some of the tools and methods that are commonly used at this stage include newsletters and flyers; information sessions and town hall meeting; information open houses at the organization's offices and/or the proposed site of the project; e-bulletins and social media updates; and community events.[25]

Events and meetings are an important part of any engagement and consultation process and the consultation plan should include a schedule of consultation events and related communications established with reference to milestones in the project planning process and other activities in the community that either complement or potentially conflict with the schedule. Some of the questions to ask and answer with respect to events and meetings include the following:[26]

---

[24] *Corporate Social Responsibility Processes and Practices Manual: Operating Guidelines* (Africa Oil Kenya B.V., July 2015).

[25] A Guide to Engaging the Community in Your Project, http://artscapediy. org/Creative-Placemaking-Toolbox/Who-Are-My-Stakeholders-and-How-Do-I-Engage-Them/A-Guide-to-Engaging-the-Community-in-Your-Project.aspx

[26] Id.

- What languages are spoken in the community? How can the organization make sure that print and other forms of communication are accessible to as many community members as possible?
- What physical barriers might prevent community members from participating in engagement and consultation opportunities (e.g., persons with disabilities, seniors, and other community members who might have difficulty accessing public transit to attend events and meetings) and how can these barriers be addressed by the organization?
- What is the best location for a meeting or event? Is it well known, accessible by public transit, physically accessible, and in an area generally regarded as "safe"?
- What is the best time of day for a meeting or event? Organizations should always consider the difficulties that local community members with jobs outside the area will have in attending daytime events. The organization should also consider the needs of caregivers and parents, seniors, those reliant on limited public transit, and others for whom daytime meetings or events might be more accessible.
- What is the tone of the organization's meeting, event, or other form of communication? Is it friendly, welcoming, and informative or full of jargon and difficult to understand?
- What other established organizations in the community can help encourage people to attend and/or "host" a meeting or event?

As mentioned above, consultation is also the best way for the organization to *gather input from the community and gain an understanding of community needs and issues*. This type of input improves the project development process and also allows the organization to gain the benefits of ideas that community members might have for the project. When obtaining input from the community, it is a good idea to have a framework for the project already in mind so that community members can comment on specific elements, as opposed to simply providing more general feedback. Tools and methods commonly used at this stage include interviews, focus groups, and roundtable discussions; small group workshops; e-mail and Web surveys; and full-day intensive meetings with local governmental officials and other community leaders.[27]

In some cases, the traditional methods of consultation will be supplemented by additional steps to build a sense of commitment within the community to the success of the project. For example, the organization may select representatives from the community to participate in the governance of the project, perhaps serving as members of the board of directors or advisory council for the project. These actions demonstrate to the community that the organization is serious about proactive and meaningful community participation in the project and makes the community feel that it has a real ownership stake in the project. However, care must be taken in developing the process for selecting the community representatives, taking into account the community's own political landscape. In addition to having community members serve on the governing board, organizations can provide for community representation on committees established to oversee certain operations and other activities of the project. Project memberships, if affordable and readily accessible to everyone in the community who is interested, may also be created. Taken together, integrating the community into governance and day-to-day management of projects builds an important sense of community stewardship.[28]

Recording the Results of the Consultation Process

Consultation involves a lot of time and effort and it is important for the organization to take the time to organize the information collected during the consultation process into a detailed compilation of the activities that can be used as a model for subsequent consultation activities and serve as a record of community engagement prior to commencement of the project. The format of the compilation will depend on the specific consultation activities but organizations should generally plan on organizing minutes and others notes of community meetings, setting aside letters and e-mails exchanged during the consultation process, and transcribing notes of interviews. Video and audio records of meetings and events should

---

[27] Id.
[28] Id.

also be preserved; however, care must be taken to ensure that appropriate permissions from community members have been obtained for the use of their images.

Obviously, one of the goals of the consultation process is to assist the organization in making decisions about whether or not to process with a project and, if the project does go forward, how much of the input from the community should be incorporated into the design of the project. The organization should schedule a specific window of time for considering all community input, perhaps extending the period in cases where further information is required on a specific issue or problem. While organizations rarely incorporate all of the ideas received from the community during the consultation process, it is important for the organization to seriously consider how the community is likely to measure the success and impact of the project. Good projects are aligned with the stated priorities of the community regarding needs and community views as to how the organization can best assist in addressing those needs. As such, one by-product of the consultation process should be a set of impact measures that conform to the priorities of the community.

Reporting to Community Members on the Consultation Process

Once the decision is made, a report on the use and impact of community input should be prepared and made available to community members in an appropriate manner. In many cases, the report will be in the form of a list of the main findings from the consultation process that includes the results of surveys that the organization may have taken that provide valuable information for other groups within the community as well as a foundation for the organization's decisions. The report should also describe the final design of the project as approved by the governing board of the organization and the plans for implementation. While reports for small projects may be disseminated by e-mail and/or posted on the organization's website, projects for which the consultation process has been lengthy and extensive should be reported on in larger interactive events such as an open house or town hall event with the expectation that additional questions from the community will need to be addressed at that time.

Community Consultation and Operational Projects

Community consultation should not be limited to traditional philanthropic and community investment activities but should be extended to
include any operational decisions that are likely to have an adverse impact
on social, environmental, and/or economic conditions in the community.
For example, the tidal wave of new technology companies in San Francisco
and Palo Alto, many of which offer free in-house meals for their employees, has disrupted the local restaurant markets in those cities and made it
difficult for smaller restaurants that had previously flourished to compete
and stay in business. These small businesses are suffering due to the loss of
business caused by employees staying in their offices to eat and are being
asked to shoulder higher and higher costs of neighborhood infrastructure,
including traffic, by local governments catering to the technology companies. Smaller restaurants are also seeing their leases terminated, rather than
extended, at the end of their term by landlords eager to convert their space
to more lucrative commercial office use. All this means that when companies are considering offering meals to their employees or adding more office
space in a neighborhood with a history of community-owned businesses
they need to engage and consult with neighborhood groups.[29]

A similar situation where the consultation process can be used to
manage and, if possible, diffuse potential disharmony between the company and its community is when community groups have complained
about how the company's operations have adversely impacted the environment surrounding the company's facilities. For example, certain types
of business activities invariably generate noise and raise safety issues, even
in the best of circumstances, and companies may need to address the concerns of community groups through an appropriate form of consultation
process that allows the community to air its grievances and facilitates discussions between the company and the community on ideas that might
mitigate the problem. Working through a facilitator, the company and
community leaders may be able to settle on practical short-term fixes,
such as limiting certain activities that are particularly noisy and/or which

---

[29] For further discussion, see Perlrothsept, N. 2016. "How Tech Companies Disrupted Silicon Valley's Restaurant Scene." *New York Times*, September 18, 2016, B1.

disrupt traffic patterns, to a small and fixed window of time each day. At the same time, the company can commit to working on new operational methods that will, as time goes by, permanently reduce safety risks (and hopefully provide cost savings to the company).[30]

When engaging in community investment activities and planning and launching for local projects, companies need to have a clear, predictable, and transparent process that is understood by all stakeholders to address issues that may arise such as establishing effective community engagement and grievance mechanisms, hiring local labor, and sourcing products and services from businesses in local communities. The activities within the process will vary depending on the stage of the investment; however, at each point the company should consider the appropriate steps with respect to planning and management, social impact assessment, engagement of community stakeholders, grievance mechanisms, identifying and executing specific community investment projects, local hiring, and procurement and management systems and reporting.[31]

Planning and Management

Companies should create and staff a corporate social responsibility (CSR) field team to oversee all aspects of engagement with local communities and understand and manage community issues through consultations with key stakeholders, promotion of information flow between the company, and the community and reporting to senior management to ensure that they understand emerging risks and concerns and allocate resources to address and mitigate any such risks. The CSR team should be led by a stakeholder engagement manager who will be responsible for managing team performance, leading engagement activities with all stakeholders, addressing day-to-day grievances that may arise, liaising with the leaders of the operations teams for operational projects that are being conducted in the community and managing local hiring and sourcing programs.

---

[30] *Engage Your Community Stakeholders: An Introductory Guide for Businesses.* (Network for Business Sustainability, 2012), 4.
[31] *Corporate Social Responsibility Processes and Practices Manual: Operating Guidelines* (Africa Oil Kenya B.V., July 2015).

Key members of the CSR team include community liaison officers (CLOs) and community development officers (CDOs).

In explaining how it used CSR teams, Africa Oil Kenya (AOK) described CLOs as representatives that are hired from the local community to act on behalf of the company to understand and manage community issues and relationships and promote communication between the company and the community. CDOs should also be hired from the local communities to assume responsibility for identifying, planning, and implementing community development projects that meet the needs of community members and build trust between the company and the community. When companies are engaged in operational projects that involve significant numbers of local personnel, the CSR team may also provide "embedded," or on-site, CLOs who work at the project site to ensure good labor relations between the company and local employees, thus contributing to the reputation of the company in the community. The roles and responsibilities of the CLOs, CDOs, and members of the operations team should be carefully and clearly defined in the stakeholder engagement plan.[32]

Social Impact Assessments

Every significant operational project should be preceded by a social impact assessment (SIA), which has been described as essential to understanding how operational activities may affect stakeholders and ensuring that appropriate management measures are put into place to minimize negative impacts.[33] The goals and purposes of an SIA, which is often conducted in parallel with an environmental impact assessment (EIA), is to develop a detailed understanding of socioeconomic context and prioritized list of risks and potential impacts that may arise. With this information, strategies can be developed and implemented to mitigate and/or minimizing negative impacts. In those cases where negative impacts are unavoidable, the SIA is an important step in determining compensation

---

[32] Id.

[33] Portions of the discussion of social impact assessments in the text are adapted from *Corporate Social Responsibility Processes and Practices Manual: Operating Guidelines* (Africa Oil Kenya B.V., July 2015).

that might be offered to adversely impacted members of the community. Some of the elements of an effective SIA include the following: it provides a comprehensive and detailed assessment of potential socioeconomic risks to impacted communities as it relates to key operations; it is carried out by assessors that have demonstrated experience in conducting thorough SIAs; it provides detailed quantitative and qualitative information on the type and nature of actual and potential impact on communities; it prioritizes potential risks based on type, nature, significance, and likelihood of impact; it helps to outline a clear stakeholder engagement plan; it generates stakeholder mapping and a list of stakeholders engaged along with contact information; and it informs grievance mechanism.

While every situation is different, it can generally be expected that a comprehensive SIA can extend for two to three months, thus requiring a high level of advance planning and coordination between the company's CSR team, which should be primarily responsible for the SIA, and other parts of the organization focusing on the operational aspects of the proposed project. As mentioned above, the SIA can be conducted alongside the EIA in order to leverage available resources and minimize the repeat surveying of community; however, the determination of how and when the two assessments are carried out will depend on whether a single assessor team has the capacity to conduct both assessments to a high standard. As for the selection of the assessor team, it is essential to identify a qualified and reputable provider that can provide assurances that all of the necessary data will be captured and that the assessment report will be credible and readily accepted among community members. In order to ensure independence and competence, the selection of an assessment team should be made only after a rigorous request for proposal (RFP) process has been completed under the supervision of the CSR team.

The SIA process involves several phases, beginning with determining the appropriate scope of the assessment in order to ensure that the most relevant data is captured and that the entire process flows efficiently. The assessment team should visit the area where the site where the planned operations project will be conducted in order to make a preliminary assessment of potential issues. Thereafter, attention should turn to a detailed collection of quantitative and qualitative data based on formal terms of reference that should have been developed while the assessment team was being selected and which lays out all the information thought to be necessary in order for the assessment to yield the required data. While the terms of reference can be based on the RFP, the final version should be carefully prepared with the assessment team to ensure that the parties are aligned as to the deliverables from the assessment process. Data can be collected in a variety of ways including surveys, observations, interviews, and structured consultations with community members, and the intention should be to record the potential impacts of the project (i.e., which communities are affected, how many people, and the nature of community dynamics). Where appropriate, such as when a proposed project is like to affect indigenous peoples and/or require potential relocation of communities, a separate human rights impact assessment should be conducted using terms of reference that have been customized to focus on human rights issues and risks.

Support for the assessment effort should be provided by both the CSR and operations teams, each of which have specific, albeit related, responsibilities during the entire process. Collaboration should begin at the RFP stage when the operations team informs the CSR team of the planned operational dates and activities and the CSR team uses that information to run the RFP process and develop the terms of reference that will provide the foundation for the assessment. With respect to determining the scope of the assessment, members of the operational team should be available for interviews and the operations team should make operational procedures and policies available to the assessment team for review. As the assessment moves forward to completion, operational team members should continue to be accessible to the assessment team and should review the final assessment report to verify data and gain familiarity with the key issues and impacts of the project and the proposed strategies for addressing those impacts during the project.

Once the collection of information through the SIA process has been completed, the results should be used to inform management decisions, and operational activities. Specifically, the CSR team should identify strategies to implement recommendations for improving impact management, working with teams to implement new practices as required. The results of the SIA, including the strategies for implementation that have been selected, should be communicated to the members of the community and local governmental authorities in order to demonstrate transparency and support ongoing community engagement. An impact management plan should be developed and monitored on an ongoing basis as the project moves forward through formal impact monitoring systems, and members of the operations team should be responsible for communicating potential issues to the CSR team and participating in the monitoring and remediation process.

Engagement Activities

Engagement activities used by AOK in communities where it proposed to engage in seismic and drilling activities included establishing a Project Stakeholder Committee (PSC) with clearly defined roles, responsibilities, and expectations to represent community interests and ensure that all critical voices are heard, including the traditionally marginalized and vulnerable.[34] Members of the PSC should be elected publicly in a transparent setting and the company should hold smaller meetings in the areas from which elected members are from in order to observe how the member interacts with his or her peers and validate that he or she is indeed a fair and trusted representative of the community. In addition to the PSC and its activities, companies should plan out an engagement strategy that ensures that all segments of the community will be regularly contacted and given an opportunity to express their concerns and describe their needs and expectations from the company and its projects. Regular contacts with local government officials are also important.

Meetings with stakeholders during the engagement process should be carefully planned to ensure that community members are aware of the meeting and have access to the tools necessary to engage properly with the company. The company should be sure that each meeting includes updates of progress on addressing specific community issues, as well as the status of the underlying project. The proceedings of stakeholder meetings, including stakeholder issues and company responses, should be fully documented and records should be maintained of attendance and the information provided at meetings. Minutes and other

---

[34] *Corporate Social Responsibility Processes and Practices Manual: Operating Guidelines* (Africa Oil Kenya B.V., July 2015).

reports of meeting should made readily available for disclosure to all interested parties and should be reviewed and approved by the company and members of the PSC.

While the CSR team is responsible for organizing and conducting engagement activities, members of the operations team should be expected to encourage local stakeholders to participate in the engagement activities and operations team representatives should attend stakeholder meetings to provide status reports and assist in addressing questions that are directly related to events that occurred at project sites. The operations team should also provide the CSR team with reports on the dynamics of activities at the project site and any interactions between operations personnel and community members outside of the regular engagement process. One important area in which both the CSR and operations teams can contribute is ensuring that adequate health, safety, and environment (HSE) safeguards are in place at operational project sites to protect local works and members of the community who live and/or work in close proximity to those sites. Among other things, a community HSE program should include sensitizing community members to potential health and safety risks associated with operations and the materials that are being used at operational sites and implementing emergency procedures.[35]

Grievance Mechanisms

Even in the best of circumstances, issues and problems will arise with stakeholders during the engagement process and it is important to anticipate these situations in advance by establishing appropriate grievance mechanisms as part of the stakeholder engagement plan with the input of stakeholder representatives who can inform the company about the most appropriate manner for addressing disputes in the community. AOK advised that the following key principles should be followed in preparing and implementing grievance mechanisms as part of the stakeholder engagement process: accessibility (i.e., stakeholders are aware of the grievance mechanisms and are able to access them without barriers such as language, finance, etc.); legitimacy (i.e., perceived as trustworthy and fair by

---

[35] Id.

stakeholder groups); predictability (i.e., provide a clear and known procedure that can be readily monitored and which is based on a time frame for each stage and clarity on the types of process and outcome it can (and cannot) offer); transparency (i.e., keep parties informed about progress and provide sufficient information about the process to build confidence in its effectiveness); equitability (i.e., ensuring that aggrieved parties have reasonable access to sources of information, advice, and expertise necessary to engage in a grievance process on fair, informed, and respectful terms); and rights comparability (i.e., ensuring that outcomes and remedies accord with internationally recognized human rights). Grievance mechanisms should be created based on strong dialogue with local communities and outcomes of grievance procedures should be documented for future reference.[36]

AOK provided suggestions on how to implement effective grievance mechanisms, based on its experiences in communities in which it conducted significant operational projects. The first step is to consult with community leaders to identify grievance mechanisms that would be appropriate given local culture and norms. Once the mechanisms have been selected, the required tools (e.g., forms) should be developed and training should be provided to personnel who will be involved in the grievance processes. Once the grievance mechanisms are ready to launch, their availability should be communicated and promoted throughout the local community and various channels for communicating grievances should be created such as suggestion boxes located outside of the offices of the operational project team, communications through members of the project stakeholder committee, a dedicated voice mailbox for people to leave information, and numbers and e-mail. AOK recommended that a formal, reliable, and transparent procedure for addressing grievance be created and maintained including acknowledgment and recording of all grievances, a commitment to provide feedback within a specified period, and recording of all grievance resolutions that is shared regularly with leaders of both the CSR and operational teams and with community stakeholders. Responsibility for AOK's grievance mechanisms was given

---

[36] Id.

to the CSR team; however, the CSR team was encouraged to involve the operations team as needed in order to understand the nature of a particular grievance and implement resolutions.[37]

Community Investment

One of the most important and impactful ways in which company can engage with the communities in which they operate is through community investment projects that are consistent with the company's overall CSR priorities and goals. Many companies launch community investment projects that are focused on improving the infrastructure in the community, which admittedly likely have business benefits to the company as well, economic development, and providing opportunities for sustainability livelihoods to community members. There is no doubt that the universe of potential community investment projects will extend much farther than the available resources of any one company; therefore, it is important for companies to approach community investment decisions strategically and take into account the factors such as potential impact, sustainability, factors for success, the business case, budget, and timeline and, of course, the relationship to the operation project.[38]

Every community investment project is different; however, in all cases the company should begin the process by completing a social impact assessment of the local community in order to identify potential investment projects and the priority issues within the community that might be suitable for company involvement given its core competencies and other available resources. As part of the social impact assessment, the company should consult with local stakeholders on potential areas for community investment projects. During the consultation process, the company should be clear with community members about the criterion that the company will be applying to determine whether a proposed project is viable and make sure that community stakeholders understand that the company has limited resources and cannot support every project, regardless of how worthy it might be. Local stakeholders will often not have the resources

---

[37] Id.

[38] Id.

and experience to submit formal proposals and the company's CSR team should assume responsibility for describing and analyzing potential projects based on the factors listed above so that further discussions can occur with stakeholders and senior management of the company, acting with input from the team conducted operational activities in the community, can make informed decisions about which projects to support. Once a project has been mutually agreed upon by the company and community stakeholders, documentation should be created that covers the company's proposed contributions and the roles and responsibility of the company, community participants, and any implementation partners. Progress of each project should be regularly monitored and reports issued to senior management of the company and community stakeholders (reports can be free-standing and/or integrated into the company's other sustainability reporting activities). Assuming that companies have multiple community investment projects in operation at any given time, a database of all such projects should be maintained, updated, and readily available for review by interested parties.[39]

Local Sourcing and Hiring

One of the most effective ways to link operational activities and community investment and engagement is through sourcing and hiring of local labor and using local vendors for materials required for operations project. Success in this area depends on close cooperation between the CSR and operations team with respect to understanding the needs, budgets, and schedule of the operations team and the operational project; articulating employment and business opportunities to community stakeholders in a transparent, specific, and objective manner (e.g., letting stakeholders know that the expected number of people who will be hired is 20 rather than saying a large number of people will be hired); clearly communicating all relevant decision-making criteria and information regarding the process to community stakeholders to ensure transparency and accountability (e.g., preferences will be given to workers and suppliers in close proximity to the operational project and then opportunities will

---

[39] Id.

be opened up to others at the county and then national levels); understanding local context and norms relating to employment, gender issues or decisions on hiring, and consulting with local stakeholders regarding the appropriate process to follow; and drafting and signing contracts.[40]

It will be important for the operations team to provide the CSR team with sufficient notice of operational requirements so that the CSR team has time to post job advertisements and circulate requests for bids on procurement opportunities. The operations and CSR teams need to collaborate on creating quality and quantity requirements for suppliers and hosting supplier forums at which the company's sourcing policies can be discussed with members of the local business community and information can be circulated regarding the company's supplier selection process.[41] Local workers and suppliers should be trained regarding grievance mechanisms that are available to them in the event that they encounter problems while carrying out their relationships with the company. As with all other community engagement initiatives, progress with respect to local hiring and procurement should be carefully measured and reports should be issued internally and to community stakeholders. Local hiring and procurement is a dynamic process given that the needs of the company will almost certainly change as time goes by and the underlying operational project evolves.

Management Systems and Reporting

Community engagement is an important and continuously changing activity for every company and it is important to implement management systems and reporting mechanisms to keep track of progress and set and modify engagement strategies as time goes by. From a planning perspective, companies should have annual and quarterly engagement plans that include engagement visits and community consultations, community investment budgets, and formal plans for coordination between the CSR and operational teams to ensure that the CSR team understands the timeline and needs from the operational side. Internal reporting and

---

[40] Id.

[41] Id.

management systems allow for assessment of progress and seamless transfer of information throughout the organization and to new staff. One part of the internal management system should be a robust orientation program for people who are joining the CSR and ongoing training for all members of the CSR team. Reports summarizing community engagement activities should be prepared no less frequently than monthly to cover key achievements; goals for the next reporting period; emerging stakeholder issues to be monitored and mitigation strategies; data on local sourcing, employment, and community investment/development projects; and grievances (number received, number resolved, analysis of trends). A records retention system for all documents, files, and other materials related to the community engagement process should also be established.[42]

Strategic Selection of Community Engagement Approaches

Organizations can choose from among multiple approaches to community engagement and will often be used two or different approaches at any given time with the same stakeholder. Selecting among community engagement approaches should be done strategically and based on guidelines that can readily be referred to in order to determine which approach (or collection of approaches) would be most suitable to a particular situation or project. According to the Network for Business Sustainability, businesses should take a systematic approach to engaging with community stakeholders that includes getting to know the community (i.e., identifying stakeholders and their issues and expectations); choosing the most appropriate engagement strategy or strategies after prioritizing stakeholders and identifying the best ways to engage with each of them; planning the engagement process, which requires identifying specific engagement processes and techniques and managing the process; and making community engagement a permanent part of the businesses' presence in the community by sharing information and continuously improving.[43]

---

[42] Id.

[43] Id. at 5.

The first step in community engagement should be identifying and prioritizing each of the groups, or stakeholders, in or related to the community that should or may wish to have a voice in the company's activities. Community stakeholders are, in effect, groups of individuals within the community who are linked in certain ways such as by issues (i.e., people concerned with the same community issue, such as public education or mass transportation); identity (i.e., people who share a set of beliefs, values, or experiences related to a specific issue such as the environment or public health); interaction (i.e., people who are linked by a set of social relationships); and geography (i.e., people who live, work, and/or shop in the same area within the community).[44] In any given community, the range of stakeholders will typically include neighborhoods, community development groups, environmental organizations, development organizations, citizen associations, nongovernmental organizations (NGOs), local nonprofit organizations, local regulators and governmental officials, other businesses in the community, indigenous peoples, and underrepresented groups in the community.[45]

Putting a list of community stakeholders together for any particular company should begin with each of the categories described above and then the search should expand to include other groups or organizations that have already reached out to the company (or in communications published within the community via newspapers or the Internet) to provide ideas, seek support, or make suggestions or complaints regarding a company activity. Actual past interactions between companies and community groups, and the topics of those interactions, provide valuable clues as to where future engagement activities should be focused. In addition, however, companies need to be careful about paying too much attention to the "squeaky wheel" in the community and ignoring the legitimate concerns of individuals and groups who are unable to put together a visible and effective public advocacy campaign with respect to their needs and interests. The company's list of community stakeholders should include the name of the stakeholder group and its mission, the contact person for the stakeholder, and personal and

---

[44] Id. at 3.
[45] Id.

professional information on other key leaders within the stakeholder, the known and anticipated issues and expectations of the stakeholder related to the company, and any history of communications and/or other interactions between the company and the stakeholders (e.g., conflicts, partnerships etc.).[46]

A company's initial list of past, current, and potential community stakeholders will generally be quite lengthy and although extensive community engagement can provide significant benefits to a company, there are obviously limits in terms of time and other resources. As such, companies need to prioritize their community stakeholders by scoring each of them on a scale of one to five (one being "strongly disagree," three being "neutral," and five being "strongly agree") on the following fundamental factors:[47]

- The stakeholder's issue/expectation is legitimate.
- The stakeholder's issue/expectation may be considered legitimate by other stakeholders (e.g., the media, NGOs, politicians, insurers, investors, distributors etc.) regardless of whether or not the company believes it to be legitimate or material.
- The stakeholder can directly impact the company due to its size, political and/or economic influence, business relationship, or otherwise.
- The stakeholder represents a vulnerable and/or underrepresented group within the community.
- The stakeholder's issue/expectation is directly related to the company's current core business activities and/or reasonably anticipated new strategic business activities.
- The stakeholders' issue/expectation is directly related to the company's announced mission, goals, and objectives with respect to community engagement.
- The stakeholder's issue/expectation is directly related to the activities of the company's suppliers or sector.

---

[46] Id. at 7.
[47] Id. at 8.

Once the list of potential community stakeholders has been prioritized, attention turns to selecting the most appropriate and potentially effective engagement strategy for the listed stakeholders, beginning with those stakeholders that have been identified as "high priority." This is the point in the process where companies should choose from among the levels of community engagement recommended by various experts, such as the International Association for Public Participation (IAP2) framework that is described elsewhere in this chapter or the following three options that have been endorsed by the Network for Business Sustainability:[48]

- Community investment ("giving back"), which is similar to community outreach and education in the IAP2 framework and features one-way communications with many community partners and occasional interactions all intended primarily to transfer information from the company to the community using a process controlled by the company. Typical activities include information sessions, charitable donations, and employee volunteering.

- Community involvement ("building bridges"), which is similar to community consultation in the IAP2 framework and features two-way communications with many community partners and repeated interactions all intended primarily to transfer information from the community to the company using a process controlled by the company. Typical activities include dialogue, consultation, and cause marketing.

- Community integration ("changing society"), which is similar to community collaboration in the IAP2 framework and features two-way communications with a select few of the highest priority community stakeholders and frequent interactions to jointly generate new information using a process in which control is jointly shared by the parties. Hallmarks of this type of engagement include joint project management and joint decision making.

---

[48] Id at 4 and 9.

According to the Network for Business Sustainability, settling on the most appropriate engagement strategy for a particular stakeholder depends on answering the following:[49]

- Are the stakeholder's expectations well understood and accepted by the company?
- Does the stakeholder consider itself to be poorly understood by the company?
- Is the stakeholder's perception of the issue inaccurate or in need of improvement?
- Has the stakeholder expressed a desire for engagement or is likely that the stakeholder would welcome engagement if approached?
- Have the reasonable expectations of the stakeholder not been met to the stakeholder's satisfaction?
- What is the current potential for deep collaboration with the stakeholder and would the stakeholder be interested in deeper collaboration?
- What is the current availability/potential for an economically viable solution to the most pressing concerns of the stakeholder that can also be easily publicized?

In general, community investment, outreach, and education is likely the best engagement strategy for a particular stakeholder when the stakeholder's expectations are understood and accepted by the company, the stakeholder's perception of the issue is inaccurate or could be improved, the potential for collaboration is low, and/or an economically viable solution exists and needs to be publicized. This basic level of engagement makes sense when a stakeholder is confused about an issue or an economically viable solution to an issue is already available and there is less need for the discovery phases associated with the other two levels of engagement. In addition, companies may offer information and education as a simple way to begin breaking down mistrust of the company by the

---

[49] Id. at 9–10.

stakeholder and lay a foundation for more extensive engagement once the stakeholder has more information about the company and its community-related objectives.

Best practices with respect to community investment, outreach and education include:

- Provide clear, instructive information, accessible to all stakeholders
- Reach the greatest number of stakeholders by using a variety of information and communication techniques
- Consider local realities and use language that will be understood by communities
- Be transparent and present factual information
- Explain the uncertainties and limits of the project; present several different scenarios
- Be open to feedback

Common techniques include brochures and flyers, advertisements, information kiosks, press releases, newsletters, door-to-door, information sessions, and financial support.[50]

Community involvement and consultation is likely the best engagement strategy for a particular stakeholder when the stakeholder's expectations are *not* well understood by the company, the stakeholder considers itself to be poorly understood, the potential for cooperation is average or higher, and/or an economically viable solution seems possible. The highest level of engagement, community integration and collaboration, is not feasible unless the company and the stakeholder understand and accept each other's expectations regarding the relationship based on two-way consultation the involves negotiation and clarification of expectations on both sides. Companies cannot, and should not, assume that they know exactly what each stakeholder expects from the company with respect to its activities in the community.

---

[50] Id. at 11.

Best practices with respect to community involvement and consultation include:

- Set up forums where stakeholders can express their views on the project and/or the company's activities
- Create informal places where the company can discuss stakeholders' concerns with them
- Guide the discussion in order to facilitate dialogue and create a synergy among participants
- Encourage stakeholders to participate within a climate of creativity, frankness, and spontaneity

Common techniques include surveys, studies, interviews, consultative committees, interactive websites, public hearings, and neutral forums.[51]

Finally, community integration and collaboration is feasible when the expectations of the particular stakeholder have not been met to their satisfaction using other engagement strategies, the stakeholder believes that it can gain from integration and collaboration and the potential for collaboration is high and an economically viable solution is not currently available or is problematic. The integration and collaboration strategy is particularly effective when the object is to develop an economically viable solution to a community issue and the parties are both highly motivated and able to bring unique resources and experiences to the table in order to address and resolve the issue and develop a long-term strategy for implementing the solution (e.g., a new community organization dedicated to the issue and solution initially sponsored by the company and co-managed by representatives of community stakeholders).[52] Not surprisingly,

---

[51] Id. at 11.

[52] The Network for Business Sustainability described a hypothetical situation of a Latin American mining company seeking to address water quality near its mine with the assistance of local stakeholders and explained that local stakeholders were eager to get involved and share their extensive knowledge of local water systems to address a complex issue. In that instance, a potential output of the integration and collaboration process would be the joint creation of a participatory management board by the company and the community to promote shared responsibility for water quality. Id. at 9.

engagement at this level should be attempted sparingly given that it will require significant investments of time and resources and carries more risk along with opportunities for real change and impact.

Best practices with respect to community integration and collaboration include developing routine that engage the community in the company's strategic planning processes and make sure employees are familiar with them and integrating solutions by concerned stakeholders into the company's decision-making processes. Common techniques include project management, strategic local or regional partnerships, sector discussion groups, joint brainstorming, conflict resolution, and work groups.[53]

In order to plan effectively for engagement and balance scarce resources companies should prepare and use a chart for project management planning that includes the following information for each of the stakeholders that are to be engaged with in some way during the planning period:[54]

- The name of the stakeholder group and its mission
- The contact person for the stakeholder and personal and professional information on other key leaders within the stakeholder
- The known and anticipated issues and expectations of the stakeholder related to the company
- Any history of communications and/or other interactions between the company and the stakeholders (e.g., conflicts, partnerships etc.).
- Relative prioritization of the stakeholder among all other company stakeholders
- Engagement strategy or strategies (i.e., investment, involvement, and/or integration)
- Potential practices or techniques for engagement
- Performance measures
- Resources (staff and budgetary)

---

[53] Id. at 11.
[54] Id. at 13.

- Timeline
- Actions taken to date
- Future actions for engagement

Community engagement is important for a specific project; however, it should not be a "one off" and companies should be prepared to design and implement a permanent engagement process with the stakeholder that facilitates continuous sharing of knowledge and improvement. Knowledge about the engagement process should be shared inside the company, and in the community, in order to develop capacity among all involved persons. Internal knowledge sharing, including creation of permanent records of prior engagement, can be tremendously valuable as people move on so that their experience is not totally lost and that there is continuity in the relationships with key stakeholders. Knowledge sharing also bakes in the practice of keeping the community informed so that there is always a current foundation for consultation and integration. Finally, for key stakeholders there should always be a plan for regular review of the relationship in order to measure progress, establish new goals, and integrate new engagement techniques.[55]

Selecting Community Engagement Tools

Effective community engagement can only be achieved if the appropriate engagement tools are selected and used in the proper manner. When selecting engagement tools, companies must create a portfolio that is timely, accessible, and appealing, inclusive, community-focused, interactive, flexible, and cost-effective. As technology has evolved, the range of engagement tools has expanded enormously. The State of Queensland Australia prepared an extensive list of potential engagement tools that included descriptions and information on benefits, considerations, and suitability for specific levels of engagement for each of the following: print materials, advertisements, media releases, websites, e-mail feedback, information hotline, town hall meetings, telephone surveys, one-on-one meetings, public displays, small group meetings, community events, charrettes, steering

---

[55] Id. at 12.

groups, community reference groups, citizen panels, engagement apps, social media, digital video, online survey tools, hard copy surveys and questionnaires, online polling, online deliberative forums, gamification, virtual reality, mixed reality, animation software, data visualization software, 3D modeling, online polling, social media monitoring, zone cards, hackathons, expert panel, online workshop, community workshop, community radio, blogs, market research, community summit, and information maze.[56]

The portfolio of engagement tools needs to accomplish a variety of things including raising awareness of the issue and informing community members of the company's interest and intent to engage; gathering information from the community, with the expectation that the type of information required may change over the course of the engagement process as the company's level of engagement shifts; and accommodating the requirements of the specific level of engagement that is occurring at the present moment (e.g., the amount and type of company resources required for engagement will change when the process moves from "informing" to setting up substantial and complex partnership arrangements with community groups and other organizations). The choice of appropriate engagement tools for the then-current level of engagement is crucial and companies often need to put together a different combination of tools if the ones originally selected are not delivering a successful engagement process. The following list of questions prepared by the State of Queensland Australia is intended to help businesses to determine how to select engagement tools best suited to achieve the critical success factors for a particular engagement project:[57]

- *Has the company considered tools that inform the community and key stakeholders from the beginning of the engagement process?* Information should be made available to the

---

[56] *Community Engagement Toolkit for Planning* (The State of Queensland Australia: Department of Infrastructure, Local Government and Planning, August 2017), 33–43.

[57] *Community Engagement Toolkit for Planning* (The State of Queensland Australia: Department of Infrastructure, Local Government and Planning, August 2017), 30–32.

community throughout the engagement process and the higher levels of engagement cannot be carried out effectively unless there is a baseline understanding of the issue and the company's initial goals and objectives with respect to the engagement process.

- *Has the company considered tools that will help build and secure a positive relationship, and the time that it might take to build this relationship?* This will include tools that create opportunities for conversations with community members, and to listen to them.
- *Has the company considered tools that will help community members contribute in a way that influences outcomes?* It is important to time the implementation of these tools so that engagement occurs when the community has the best opportunity to influence outcomes.
- *Has the company considered tools that will allow conversations about strategic planning to continue after the planning scheme is developed?* Continuing the conversation will build community capacity to contribute to the next planning scheme engagement process.
- *Has the company considered tools that will be accessible to all stakeholder groups and community members, so that they are informed about the engagement process and encouraged to participate?* Accessibility is essential to achieving a truly participative and inclusive engagement process and careful consideration needs to be given to the economic, social, and cultural characteristics of the target groups within the local community.
- *Has the company considered tools that are appropriate for the company's local community?* Choose tools that are accessible for the entire community, that enable the company to take the engagement process to the community and which the community is interested in using. In larger communities, this may mean a combination that includes online and social media tools for younger people and traditional print information and live meetings for community residents who do not have ready access to the Internet.

- *Has the company considered tools that provide information to stakeholders and community members in a way that is easy for them to understand?* Choose tools that present information in an easily understandable format, use plain language, and allow the company to clarify issues.
- *Has the company considered tools that encourage all sectors of the community to be involved in conversations about planning?* Choose tools that will appeal to diverse groups within the community and a cross-section of the population and that will help the company reach all community members, including those with specific needs (e.g. people with disability, older people, younger people).
- *Has the company considered tools that will help the community to make properly made submissions for use in the engagement process?* In order for the company to make sense of the input received during the engagement process, it will need to ask community members to organize their submissions in a way that can be easily understood and analyzed; however, since some community members may have trouble with complying with this request the company needs to develop tools to help them.
- *Has the company considered how good ideas can be captured as part of the process, regardless of whether they are made as part of a properly made submission?* It is important to help build community capacity to understand the issues that are being considered in the engagement process and how to express concerns in relation to these issues. It is also important to recognize community diversity and to include engagement techniques in a process that enables community members to express their ideas. Where good ideas are expressed using these techniques they should be able to influence the engagement and decision-making process, regardless of whether they are part of a "properly made" submission.
- *Has the company considered tools that encourage the entire community to participate?* Choose tools that allow the community to become involved, rather than just individuals or groups.

- *Has the company considered tools that will help community members and stakeholders understand what is in the best interests of the community, and the trade-offs that may be required to achieve the best interests of the community?* Choose tools that enable community members to explore and experiment, discuss and debate and, ultimately, understand the issues and trade-offs associated with making decisions regarding specific community issues.
- *Has the company considered tools that allow the community to consider the big picture and discuss the big picture with the company?* This could include a combination of tools that inform and provide comprehensible background information, as well as tools that allow community members to deliberate about the challenges associated with addressing a specific issue and collaboratively create potential solutions.
- *Has the company considered that a variety of different tools and techniques for engagement will be needed over time?* Different engagement tools will connect better with some communities. Where possible, use a mix of qualitative and quantitative engagement methods to capture a diverse sample of opinions.
- *Has the company considered the resources that are available, both budget and staff time, to deliver the engagement tools and techniques?* Availability and allocation of resources should be reviewed before the engagement process begins and revisited periodically as the process unfolds, particularly when the necessary level of engagement intensifies.

Engaging with Specific Groups

Engagement typically requires developing relationships with a number of different groups within the community, each of which has its own characteristics. For example, in any given engagement process a company may need to inform, consult, and/or collaborate with groups that different substantially with respect to culture, gender, age, socioeconomic background, values, language, physical and mental abilities, and needs. As such, while decisions can and should be made regarding issues and processes that would apply to every group in the engagement process, the plans for engagement will often need to be customized to ensure that all individuals and groups within the community can participate in a meaningful way without undue disruption to their lives. While consideration should be taken of the actual or potential special needs of every material community group, particular attention should be paid to indigenous peoples, elderly community members, young people, people with disabilities, ethnic and cultural minorities in a particular community and disadvantaged and homeless people.[58]

The first step in determining how best to engage with a particular community group is to identify reputable local representatives of that group to let them know about the company's intentions and seek their guidance as to how best to engage with the community members that they represent. These representatives should be able to share information and experience on the needs of the group and provide ideas from past engagement exercises as to how best to get them involved. There will often be existing community networks that can provide support for developing the capacity necessary for effective engagement with the particular groups including dissemination information and assisting with the logistics of conducting meetings and getting group members to those meetings. For example, when it is clear that the engagement process will need to involve extensive consultation with older people and/or people with disabilities the company should consider collaboration with neighborhood organizations that have the experience and special resources to facilitate participation by members of these groups.

Among the questions and issues that should be considered when designing an engagement process for a specific group is the timing and location of meetings, which should be selected based on the special requirements of individuals in the group with regard to accessibility and their job- and family-related responsibilities; selection of venues at which it will be easiest for members of the group to listen, concentrate, and

---

[58] The discussion of engaging with specific groups included herein is adapted from *Community Engagement Toolkit for Planning* (The State of Queensland Australia: Department of Infrastructure, Local Government and Planning, August 2017), 48–49.

contribute their views; setting the duration of the meetings to conform to the needs of the group, realizing that some groups are composed of individuals who need more time to express their views and others would benefit from a larger number of shorter meetings that could be fit into their schedules as workers, parents, and caregivers; and determining the optimal size of meetings, since effectively engaging with underserved groups that may otherwise be out of touch with community matters often works best when engagement is done through smaller meetings that are less intimidating and encourage more participation.

In addition to meetings, companies needs to deploy other tools to communicate with groups that might not otherwise regularly receive information regarding their communities and the specific issues that are being raised in the engagement process. For example, while many groups will respond to general advertising and newsletters, some community members are not able to receive those engagement tools and outreach to them will have to be done in other ways, often through person-to-person communications from people that are trusted by the recipients. Another obvious problem that must be considered is that many groups, such as the elderly, have difficulty using and/or accessing technology and thus cannot easily be reached through e-mail or social media. Regardless of how the information is conveyed to a particular group, it must be provided in a form that is accessible and respectful, which means arranging for appropriate translations of printed materials and audio and making sure that videos and graphics are prepared in a manner that conveys the information clearly and is free of language and material that might be culturally offensive.

In many communities, provision may have been made by local governments to require engagement and consultation with specified community groups in advance of considering and ultimately making decisions regarding a community development project. These requirements appear most often with respect to projects that will involve the development of new structures and/or impacts to the natural habitat in the community and sponsors of such a project will be required to prepare and publish an "impact report" and complete a minimum period of "waiting" before proceeding with the project during which community members can submit comments on, and raise objections to, the project. A case study of required community engagement prior to an investment/development project comes from federal, state, and local efforts to comply with the letter and spirit of the United Nations Declaration on the Rights of Indigenous Peoples (UNDRIP), which was adopted with the goal of identifying, describing, and affirming certain rights believed to be essential for preservation of indigenous peoples' identity including the right to participate in decision making.[59] Governments at all levels have struggled to implement the duties of states laid out in the UNDRIP with respect to free, prior, and informed consent, which calls on states to consult with indigenous peoples on legislative and administrative measures affecting them, such as forced relocation, culture, intellectual property, lands, territories, and resources, as well as development planning within the state, with a view to obtaining indigenous peoples' free, prior and informed consent. Clearly companies need to tread carefully and deliberately when considering investment and development projects that will impact indigenous peoples in their communities and must be sure to adhere to any formal legal standards and establish a process on their own that meets or exceeds best practices for corporate social responsibility.[60]

Developing Content for the Engagement Process

In order for the engagement process to be effective the content in the communication tools must be clear and easily understood to the intended audiences. The process of creating the content gets complicated when there are multiple community groups with different needs in terms of the information they need in order to participate. At a minimum, company must be sure that the content provides recipients with a clear understanding of the proposed project or the issue that is to be discussed during the engagement process and the goals of the company in undertaking the engagement (e.g., what decisions will the company likely be making when

---

[59] http://un.org/esa/socdev/unpfii/documents/faq_drips_en.pdf

[60] For further discussion, see Lewis, C. 2012. *Corporate Responsibility to Respect the Rights of Minorities and Indigenous Peoples*; and Implementing the UN Declaration on the Rights of Indigenous People (Inter-Parliamentary Union 2014).

the engagement process has been completed and what role the engagement process will play in those decisions). When communicating with community groups the company needs to explain to those groups exactly what role they are expected to play and what they need to do in order to be effective in that role. For example, does the company want them to read a newsletter and/or watch a video in order to become more informed about an issue and/or the company's activities or does the company want community members to attend meetings and forums. At the highest levels of engagement, the purpose of communications might be soliciting the participation of community members in a new project as volunteers and/or donors. Whatever the proposed role of the community members will be, the engagement tools must make it clear and easy for them to comply if they wish. Engagement materials should be designed in a manner that positively conveys the company's image and many companies will test their materials with a small group before broad distribution.[61]

Feedback and Reporting

Community members and groups should not be expected to participate in the engagement process unless there is a commitment from the company to compile the feedback and report to the community of what was learned and how the engagement process fit into the decisions made by the company on the specific project and on how the company might address a particular community issue in the future. Before the engagement process commences, the company needs to consider how it will follow up with the community after the process is completed, how the engagement process will be documented in a report to the community (i.e., descriptions of the objectives of the process and the participants in the process; presentation and analysis of data collected during the process; a description of how the company used the data in its decisions and the decisions that the company has made along with the reasons therefore; and a summary of future actions by the company including steps to be

---

[61] *Community Engagement Toolkit for Planning* (The State of Queensland Australia: Department of Infrastructure, Local Government and Planning, August 2017), 61.

taken to institutionalize the engagement process), and how the report will be made readily accessible to everyone in the community included those groups for which special arrangements were necessary to allow them to participate in the engagement process.[62]

Auditing and Evaluating the Engagement Process

Each engagement process should be seen as an opportunity for improvement and companies must conduct a thorough evaluation of the tools, methods, problems, and outcomes contemporaneously with the preparation of the report to the community. At that point a number of questions should be considered including the following:[63]

- Has the company considered how the engagement process addressed the core community engagement guiding principles?
- Did the engagement process ensure that the project focused on the best interests of the community?
- What engagement tools did the company use to make sure that the broader community had a voice in the process and were they successful?
- Did the company make sure that the engagement process was open, honest, and meaningful and that all community members had reasonable access to the process?
- Did the company reach out to, and encourage, all sectors of the community to become engaged?
- Was the engagement process appropriate for the community and the circumstances of the project?
- Did the engagement process include tools that enabled community members to contribute and express their ideas and influence

---

[62] Id. at 68.

[63] Adapted from *Community Engagement Toolkit for Planning* (The State of Queensland Australia: Department of Infrastructure, Local Government and Planning, August 2017), 69.

the process, regardless of whether these contributions and ideas were expressed as part of a "properly made" submission?

- Was community adequately informed early in the process?
- Was the decision-making process transparent and were community members and other participants in the engagement process provided with reasons for the decision and information on how their contributions shaped the decisions?
- Was the engagement process completed within the allocated budget?

For each question or issue, the company must have quantitative or qualitative data to support its assessment. In addition, the company must focus on what it can do better to overcome challenges and issues that came up during the engagement process and make an internal record of the process and evaluation that becomes a permanent part of the company's knowledge base and which can be shared internally with current and future members of the company's community engagement team.

In addition to contributing the proposed set of core values for the practice of public participation and community engagement described above, the IAP2 developed the IAP2 Quality Assurance Standard for Community and Stakeholder Engagement, which organizations can use to audit their engagement process against the IAP2 core values.[64] The IAP2 Quality Assurance Standard Process for Community and Stakeholder Engagement includes 11 steps, most of which has been described in some way in the sections above: program definition; agreement of purpose/context and identification of negotiables and non-negotiables; level of participation; stakeholder identification and relationship development; project requirements; development and approval of engagement plan; execution of engagement plan; feedback; evaluation and review; monitoring and documentation of evidence. With respect to evaluation and review, the IAP2 noted that it involves reviewing the engagement project to determine:

---

[64] *Quality Assurance Standard for Community and Stakeholder Engagement* (The International Association for Public Participation, May 2015).

- The extent to which engagement project requirements were identified
- Successful stakeholder identification and engagement
- Achievement of project goals and objectives
- Satisfaction levels among all stakeholders from power brokers to minority groups
- Cultural awareness of and ongoing commitment to community and stakeholder engagement
- Degree of stakeholder involvement in decision making and comparison of this against initial project positioning on the IAP2 spectrum
- Change and impact as a result of engagement outcomes
- The need for further analysis of outcomes or additional engagement activities

The audit process contemplated by the IAP2 Quality Assurance Standard Process for Community and Stakeholder Engagement is intended to assess both the compliance with the recommended process and the quality of the documentation presented as evidence of compliance. For each of the seven IAP2 Core Values for Public Participation, the IAP2 has developed a handful of indicators; standards of the level of quality for each indicator that permit distinguishing among elementary, emerging, and exemplary levels of quality; and suggestions regarding the type of evidence that should be available for use in assessing the level of quality for each indicator. For example, one of the core values requires that input from participants be sought in designing how they participate in the engagement process. The indicator for this value is a dialogue between representatives on the most suitable way of engaging participants, with assessment of quality based on demonstrating how stakeholders influenced the process for the project. Merely making assumptions on engagement techniques were made without stakeholder dialogue would be an elementary level of quality. Making reasonable efforts to seek feedback on the potential engagement process with all stakeholder groups would be an emerging level of quality. An exemplary level of quality would be when the sponsor has enabled the participants to have a key role in determining the engagement processes and techniques.

CHAPTER 4

Community Investment

Most businesses, once they reach a certain size and level of resources, provide support for activities of organizations in their communities that are dedicated to address social issues or needs in the community. There is no shortage of issues that companies can focus on in their communities. For example, among the "global challenges" identified by the Future-Fit Business Framework as being the critical environmental and social issues for businesses and society as a whole were the failure to adequately invest in, upgrade, and secure critical infrastructure, coupled with rapid and poorly planned urbanization, which has undermined the long-term health and resilience of communities; and a severe income disparity between the world's richest and poorest citizens, which both contributes to and is exacerbated by underemployment, a growing skills gap and depressed economies; social instability, which negatively impacts communities and markets and arises from a lack of equitable treatment and access to resources; and erosion of trust in institutions, from governments to business, due to unethical practices and a lack of transparency.[1] In any given community, businesses of any size can make a meaningful contribution in relatively simple ways such as supporting reading programs for young children, raising awareness of infectious diseases, and other health-related issues or providing meals to homeless people in the community.

The form of community contribution and engagement by a company can vary significantly, running from a one-time cash donation to a "good cause" to investment of cash, in-kind resources, and management time into the creation of long-term partnership with a community organization that works on a broader and deeper solution to a particular issue that has a material impact on the business and the community in

---

[1] *Future-Fit Business Framework, Part 1: Concepts, Principals and Goals* (Future-Fit Foundation, Release 1, May 2016), 11, FutureFitBusiness.org.

which it operates. While positive social and environmental impact in the community is important, businesses need not totally forego commercial advantages when supporting community organizations, as demonstrated by the popularity of "cause-related marketing" initiatives, which involve a collaboration between a business and a charity under which a product, service, or brand of the business is affiliated with a particular charitable cause and a portion of the proceeds from sales of the product, service, or brand is donated, with thoughtful publicity, to the charity.

When developing the business case for a community investment, consideration needs to be given to the potential contribution that the particular project will have as a "business driver" including benefits such as compliance with global certification requirements, competitive advantage, customer loyalty, compliance with governmental requirements, building the company's social license, risk management, reputation, access to land, and improving local workforce skills and productivity.[2] Examples include the following:[3]

- Logging firms comply with legal requirements by entering into social responsibility agreements with local communities to provide financing for social infrastructure and services in those communities.
- A company's innovative program for providing assistance to indigenous peoples in the community in which the company operates was a significant factor in the company's ability to land a significant contract.
- Companies that voluntarily join an industry sector group that has developed social responsibility principles make a public commitment to contribute to local development.
- A company creates and builds its social license to operate in a severely underdeveloped community by making long-term commitments to work directly with local stakeholders on community development programs.

---

[2] *Strategic Community Investment: A Quick Guide* (Highlights from IFC's Good Practice Handbook) (Washington DC: International Finance Corporation, February 2010), 8.

[3] Id.

- Responding to concerns about working conditions in its supply chain, a company partners with a local nongovernmental organization in a developing country to provide education on workers' rights and training and microfinancing for female entrepreneurship to provide alternative economic opportunities.
- A company launches a large HIV/AIDS program including education and financial support for health services, as well as extensive outreach within local communities, that eventually leads to dramatic workforce productive gains due to reduced mortality and absenteeism and lower health insurance premiums.

The challenge for companies is computing and assigning a value to the business drivers involved in a particular community investment project. For example, while there are costs associated with general community engagement and consultations in advance of a project (e.g., wages, communications, facilities, equipment, logistics, etc.), they must be balanced against potential benefits and avoided costs derived from completing a project ahead of schedules and avoiding contractual penalties for project delays. Additional intangible benefits include building trust and goodwill and avoiding negative effects on the company's reputation.[4]

Defining Corporate Community Investment

Philanthropy (e.g., grants, volunteering, and donations) has been a mainstay of community engagement and involvement for businesses; however, more and more attention has been focused on how businesses can contribute to their communities through innovative investment activities designed to achieve economic, social, and environment objectives. This trend has led to extensive research and guidance on social investment generally and, in the context of engaging with local communities, corporate community investment. While investing in community-focused projects involves many of the tools and principles used with traditional investments made by businesses on a day-to-day basis, there are unique issues

---

[4] Id.

and challenges that need to be considered. This section sets the stage for building the business case for deploying scarce resources in the community by introducing and explaining several useful definitions of corporate community/social investment.

LBG (http://lbg-online.net/), which is managed by Corporate Citizenship, a global corporate responsibility consultancy based in London with offices in Singapore and New York, has developed an emerging global standard for measuring corporate community investment.[5] LBG noted that while businesses engage in a wide range of activities that have a positive impact on society and contribute to sustainability including creation of wealth and jobs, delivery of goods and services, payment of taxes and support for innovation, corporate community investment can and should be distinguished. According to LBG, corporate community investment should be defined and understood as including "voluntary engagement with charitable organizations and activities that extends beyond companies' core business activities."[6]

LBG explained that two key questions need to be considered and answered affirmatively when determining is a particular contribution or activities falls into the category of corporate community investment: "Is it voluntary?" *and* "Is it charitable?"[7] As to the question of "voluntariness," the threshold is that the contribution or activity must be something that a business chooses to do and is not mandated under any legal or contractual obligation. In addition, as mentioned above, the activity should be outside of the core business activities of the company, which means that using less energy or protecting the health and safety of employees, each hallmarks of a socially responsible business, would not be considered a corporate community investment. Finally, corporate community investment does not include steps that companies should be expected to take to mitigate, or compensate community members for, the adverse environmental and

---

[5] *From Inputs to Impact: Measuring Corporate Community Contributions through the LBG Framework—A Guidance Manual* (London: Corporate Citizenship, 2014), 3. The initiative was initially referred to as the "London Benchmarking Group."

[6] Id. at 4.

[7] Id. at 3.

social impacts associated with a particular business activity undertaken in pursuit of the company's economic and financial objectives.

In order for the second condition to be satisfied, the support must be given to "an organization or activity that is recognized in its geographical location and cultural context as having a clear charitable purpose (e.g., advancing education, protecting health or supporting human rights)."[8] Contributions to formally recognized charities are the easiest to identify; however, qualifying organizations can also include nonprofits, nongovernmental organizations (NGOs), third sector, civil society, schools, universities, government departments, and social enterprises. Whether or not a particular organization meets the test turns on whether it is has a purpose, or is delivering an activity, that is broadly recognized as charitable (e.g., education) and being managed in a way so as to deliver public rather than private benefit (i.e., the organization cannot be focused on delivering financial or other returns to private parties, such as shareholders).

Examples of contributions and activities that would qualify as a corporate community contribution include a cash donation to a local registered charity; support of education through a program that allows employees to use some of their paid time to participate in a reading partnership with an inner-city school; and running a program in partnership with a charity to provide work experience and training to homeless people. Supporting the socially responsible actions of others, such as when an airline encourages passengers to donate their unused foreign currency to an international NGO when returning home from a trip abroad, also qualifies; however, the airline's reporting on this activity should separate the contributions by passengers from its own contribution so that the airline does not take undue credit beyond the value that its leverage provided to the NGO.

Businesses take many voluntary actions that have positive sustainability impacts, but they will not count as corporate community investments

---

[8] LBG pointed out that there is no single internationally agreed definition of charitable purpose and that reference needs to be made to applicable laws and guidelines relating to charities and tax-exempt charitable organizations in specific jurisdictions. For that reason, LBG focuses on the purpose of the contribution/activity (i.e., its intent and outcome) and not simply the legal status of the beneficiary. Id. at 4–5.

if the "charitable" criterion is not also satisfied. For example, monitoring waste at a company's factories is laudable but is generally considered to be focused on the company's own environmental performance and not on wider charitable benefits, even though members of the community will presumably appreciate the company's efforts. In that situation the cost of monitoring should not be included in corporate community investment but should usually fit into the company's environmental reporting.[9] Other areas in which careful assessment of whether or not a valid corporate community investment has occurred include mandatory contributions, carbon offset, responsible product use, facilitating giving by customers and/or suppliers, support for small businesses, and provision of benefits to employees and their family members.[10]

While LBG believed that the term "corporate community investment" was most descriptive, there are, not surprisingly, a number of different terms that are used to refer to the covered activities included "social investment," "community social investment," corporate social responsibility (CSR) programs, "corporate citizenship," philanthropy, "company giving," "giving back," social programs, "catalytic philanthropy," "strategic philanthropy," and creating "shared value." ISO 26000 described "community social investment" as taking place when organizations invest their resources in initiatives and programs aimed at improving social aspects of community life.[11] Community social investment includes both traditional capital investments by organizations and financial support to projects that may be identified, funded, and/or managed by other groups such as nongovernmental organizations.[12] ISO 26000 notes that organizations generally choose from among a wide array of potential community social investments including projects related to education, training, culture, health care, income generation, infrastructure development, improving access to information, or any

---

[9] Id. at 5.

[10] See specific LBG guidance notes on these areas. Id. at 5.

[11] International Organization for Standardization, ISO 26000: Guidance on Social Responsibility (Geneva, 2010), 68.

[12] *Handbook for Implementers of ISO 26000, Version Two* (Middlebury, VT: ECOLOGIA, 2011), 33.

other activity likely to promote economic or social development; however, when creating its community social investment agenda, an organization should purposefully seek to align its contribution with its core competencies and the needs and priorities of the communities in which it operates and take into account priorities set by local and national policymakers and the actions that are already being taken by other community stakeholders. ISO 26000 also emphasizes the importance of soliciting and encouraging community involvement in the design and implementation of projects to maximize success and build a foundation for projects to survive and prosper (i.e., to achieve sustainability) as the organization reduces its direct involvement.

Developing a Community Investment Strategy

Corporate philanthropy has a long tradition and companies have often been attempting various types of community investment. While these efforts are generally well meaning and have led to significant improvements in well-being in the communities in which the companies are operating, there are also signs that community investments fail to fulfill their full potential, for either the company or the community. Given that many investment projects involve significant amounts of resources, including time and goodwill, falling short on results means that employee morale may suffer and that community members lose faith and trust in the company. One list of the reasons why community investments may not achieve the goals established at the beginning included the following factors:[13]

- Limited understanding of the often complex local context
- Insufficient participation and ownership of by local stakeholders
- A perception of "giving" rather than "investing," including a lack of clear objectives

---

[13] *Strategic Community Investment: A Quick Guide* (Highlights from IFC's Good Practice Handbook) (Washington DC: International Finance Corporation, February 2010), 5.

- Detachment of the activity from core business strategy and competencies
- Responding to local requests in an ad hoc manner
- Lack of professionalism and business rigor
- Insufficient focus on sustainability
- Provision of free goods and services
- No exit or handover (to the community) strategy
- Overemphasis on infrastructure and failure to address skills and capacity building
- Lack of transparency and clear performance criteria
- Failure to measure and communicate results

Failures in any of the areas listed above can quickly overwhelm the community investment activities of any company. Managers and employees alike may complain that even though significant resources have been invested, conditions in the community do not improve and in many cases projects that have been meticulously designed and built end up abandoned or significantly underutilized. The performance and social impact of community investments also suffer when companies have no way to manage requests that come in from the community and drift off into areas that are far afield from the company's core competencies and overall mission.

While companies could abandon community investments in order to obtain relief from the challenges described above, such an approach is no longer practical or advisable for firms looking to build a sustainable business. Community engagement and involvement, including community investment, is essential for attracting talent and satisfying the expectations of customers, investors, and other stakeholders. As such, companies need to apply the same discipline to community investing that they do to all other aspects of their business and operations and this means following a deliberative process to develop a comprehensive community investment strategy that effectively deploys the company's core competencies to support community-focused projects that deliver the strongest impact given the level of investment.

The International Finance Corporation (IFC) has a keen interest in projects promise to improve conditions in communities around the world. In an effort to improve the effectiveness of these projects, the

IFC recommended the following steps for managing the developing and implementation of a community investment strategy:[14]

- Assess the overall business context to identify risks and opportunities and align the company's core competencies and internal functions with the proposed investment activities. This is the point in the process where the focus needs to be placed on developing a business case for the particular investment project that is tied to specific community investment objectives and ensuring that the company's core competencies and resources are being effectively utilized to support communities. Core business competencies can come in many different forms and may include research and development, convening power, supply chain contacts, access to consumers, business know-how, facilities, equipment, logistics, and staff time and expertise.

- Assess the local context to gain a better understanding of the social and environmental needs and issues in the community. The assessment should cover socioeconomic factors, stakeholders and networks, and potential partners for implementing the project. The goal is to link the community investment strategy to the local context and identify and describe (i.e., develop eligibility criteria) the individuals and groups within the community that will be primary targets for the proposed investments.

- Engage with the local community at each level of engagement that is necessary in order to implement the potential project. Engagement runs from one-way communications intended primarily to share information throughout the community to full consultation that allows community members to have meaningful participation in the project and, in some cases, share in the decision-making process. At a minimum, engagement supports planning and prioritization and helps

---

[14] *Strategic Community Investment: A Quick Guide* (Highlights from IFC's Good Practice Handbook) (Washington, DC: International Finance Corporation, February 2010), 4 and 7.

with managing community expectations. Engagement should extend to potential community partners that might be willing to collaborate on implementation of specific projects.

- Invest in capacity building in order to ensure that there is sufficient capital and other resources available within the community in order for the project to be sustainable. Capacity building begins with a needs assessment that identifies the types of capacities and skills required for implementing the project. The next step is to develop strategies for filling any gaps including additional investment projects that will run in parallel.

- Set parameters including goals and objectives, guiding principles, and criteria for the selection of specific investment projects; key investment areas (i.e., target groups and issues); exit/handover strategy, budget, scope, and timeline.
  The community investment strategy should extend over a three- to five-year period since many of the specific projects and initiatives will take several years to evolve before performance can be fully and fairly measured.

- Select the appropriate implementation model for the project among various alternatives such as conducting the project through an in-house community investment group, investing through an affiliated corporate community investment foundation, outsourcing implementation to a third party, creating a multistakeholder partnership, or some combination of two or more of the previously mentioned methods. For each implementation model, consideration needs to be given to decision making and governance structures.

- Measure and communicate the results of the project based on progress of appropriate indicators from baseline measures established at the beginning of the project. While return on investment is important, measurement should also take into account perceptions of community members regarding the impact of the project on their lives and the community in general and the impact of the project on company employees. Measures of impact should be reported to the community using an organized communications strategy.

Community investment strategy should be integrated with other company programs that involve individuals and groups within the community such as stakeholder engagement programs, grievance processes, local environmental and social impact management processes, and initiatives to promote local hiring and contracting. In addition, while responsibility for development of the community investment strategy may be vested in a small group, it is essential to reach out across functions and departments in order to promote cross-functional coordination and accountability for supporting the objectives of the community investment strategy. Examples of ways in which functional groups within the company may interface with communities on a regular basis include the following:[15]

- Business Development will often be the initial contact with communities
- Human Resources will be involved in recruiting and hiring employees from the local community and establishing compensation and benefits for such employees
- Land Acquisition will negotiate purchases and leases of properties in the community for business operations including resettlement and compensation
- Procurement will enter into contracts with local vendors for goods and services
- Engineering and Logistics will provide support for community investment projects that relate to infrastructure and development
- Environmental and Social Management will be involved in efforts to avoid and/or mitigate adverse environmental and social impacts of company activities and negotiate compensation for such impacts with community members.
- Community Liaison will be responsible for broader community engagement processes and grievance management.
- Government Relations will liaise and coordinate with relevant local authorities and governmental units.

---

[15] Id. at 12.

- External Relations/Communications will work with media and key external audiences and manage internal communications regarding community investments.
- Contractors will operate in communities and provide construction activities, workforce interaction, and transport/trucking.
- Security will oversee company personnel and/or outside contractors that provide security for employees and community members visiting the company's facilities and venues where community investment activities are occurring.

Cross-functional coordination is facilitated by involving each of the functions in the planning process and allows the company to leverage a wide range of resources, skills, and competencies in executing the community investment strategy. In addition, by involving all of the functions in the strategy development and implementation process, the company can avoid situations where a function inadvertently undermines community investment efforts as it carries out its normal duties and responsibilities.

Many of the ideas and guidelines mentioned above can also be found in ISO 26000, which recommends that organizations do the following relating to social investments, which is the term ISO 26000 uses to discuss community investing:[16]

- Take into account the promotion of community development in planning social investment projects, making sure that each project broadens opportunities for members of the local community (e.g., by increasing local procurement and any outsourcing so as to support local development).
- Build the capacity for collecting and sharing information in order to effectively identify, assess, negotiate, and measure the performance of investment opportunities.

---

[16] International Organization for Standardization, ISO 26000: Guidance on Social Responsibility (Geneva, 2010), 68.

- Avoid actions that perpetuate a community's dependence on the organization's philanthropic activities, ongoing presence, or support.
- Assess its own existing community-related initiatives and report to the community and to people within the organization and identify where improvements might be made.
- Consider partnering with other organizations, including government, business, or NGOs to maximize synergies and make use of complementary resources, knowledge, and skills.
- Consider contributing to programs that provide access to food and other essential products for vulnerable or discriminated groups and persons with low income, taking into account the importance of contributing to their increased capabilities, resources, and opportunities.

Companies engaging in community investing can also learn from the emerging practices of private investors and an increasing number of philanthropic groups with respect to "impact investing," which seeks both financial returns and intentional, measurable social returns.[17] One cautionary lesson is that impact investing, and thus community investment, is hard, particularly when the projects involve local groups that will need assistance in many basis business skills and activities. For-profit organizations also need to be mindful of the goals and expectations of other stakeholders, particularly investors whose primary interest is seeking "market rate" financial returns. In those situations, companies will need to reach out to and engage with stakeholders outside of their local communities to explain how community investing will be conducted and the anticipated benefits to the company and all its stakeholders.

The framework for measuring corporate community investment developed by LBG, which has been mentioned above, can be used to provide prompts for identifying and answering many of the basic questions

---

[17] To learn more about impact investing, see the information available from the Global Impact Investing Network (https://thegiin.org/impact-investing/).

that should be addressed in creating a community investment strategy.[18] The first set of questions revolve around the "inputs" from the company into the community investment initiative (i.e., how (form of contribution), why (driver for contribution), what (issue addressed), and where (location of activity)). Companies generally have the option to contribute a mix of resources including cash, time, in-kind (including pro bono), and management costs and the form of contribution will vary depending on the project and more of one of type of resource may be required at a particular point in the evolution of an investment project. While community investment is the primary topic of this chapter, companies typically also make charitable gifts and sponsor commercial initiatives in the community. When developing the business case for a community investment, consideration also needs to be given to the potential contribution that the particular project will have as a "business driver" including benefits such as compliance with global certification requirements, competitive advantage, customer loyalty, compliance with governmental requirements, building the company's social license, risk management, reputation, access to land, and improving local workforce skills and productivity.[19]

The next consideration for companies is what issues should be the focus of community investment activities. There is no shortage of issues that could be selected for the focus of attention and companies should take the opinions of local community members as expressed during the engagement process into account. Also relevant at this point are the core competencies of the company since the most effective and impactful community investment occurs when the existing resources of the company are tailored to the needs associated with a specific issue. For example, if the company is involved in the provision of health-related services and/or research and development relating to medical products, it probably makes sense for that company's community investments to be in the health

---

[18] *From Inputs to Impact: Measuring Corporate Community Contributions through the LBG Framework—A Guidance Manual* (London: Corporate Citizenship, 2014), 3.

[19] *Strategic Community Investment: A Quick Guide* (Highlights from IFC's Good Practice Handbook) (Washington, DC: International Finance Corporation, February 2010), 8.

area, such as supporting the creation of clinics in underserved neighborhoods and/or wellness-related educational programs. Other major issue areas mentioned by LBG included education, economic development, environment, arts and culture, social welfare, and emergency relief.

The second set of questions in the LBG framework relate to "outputs," which are measures of what happens in the community and in the company itself as a result of implementing a particular community investment project. Community outputs include the individuals reached/supported, the type of beneficiary, organizations supported, and other company-specific output measures (e.g., environment). Company, or "business," outputs might include employees involved in the activity, media coverage achieved, customers/consumers reached, suppliers/distributors reached, and other influential stakeholders reached. A third set of outputs, referred to as "leverage," includes additional resources funneled to a particular cause as a result of the company's community investment, which resources include funds raised from payroll giving and customers, other employee contributions, resources committed by other organizations that the company brought into a project, and personal time of employees spent volunteering for a particular project.

The final set of questions relates to the anticipated impacts of the community investment projects on the lives of community members, the skills and resources of community organizations, the local environment, the skills and morale of employees, and the well-being and strength of the business of the company. For community members, LBG challenges companies to measure the depth and type of impact (e.g., did the community investment lead to improvement in skills and/or the quality of life of a significant percentage of the target community members). The impact of a community investment on organizations in the community can be in the form of improved or new services, increased capacity to reach more people or spent more time with clients, improved management processes, increased profile, and capacity to take on more staff or volunteers. In addition to impacts on the environment, consideration should be given impacts on environmental behavior. Improvements to job-related skills of employees as well improvements in the personal well-being from participating in the community investment activity are valuable outcomes for the company. Finally, the business of the company itself may be improved through human resources benefits, improvements in relations with community members and other stakeholders, and the perception of the company in the eyes of such parties, generation of new business opportunities, operational improvements, and uplift in brand awareness.

Approaches to Community Investment

Tran, in an article prepared for the quarterly publication of Social Ventures Australia, argued that the businesses should use a combination of social investment approaches as part of a well-managed portfolio in order to deliver greater impact, support the generation of social and business value in different ways, and engage different stakeholders.[20] The portfolio approach would include initiatives and activities from among four categories: traditional philanthropy, engaged philanthropy, catalytic philanthropy, and "creating shared value."[21]

According to Tran and others, adapting a range of approaches can provide a number of benefits and advantages to businesses including appealing to different sets of stakeholders; achieving a broader set of social and business outcomes; diversifying the risk in achieving the social and business objectives; making use of a wider range of skill sets across the organization; taking advantage of different available opportunities and forming nontraditional alliances; and designing complementary initiatives that increase the overall impact of the portfolio. In most cases, businesses make changes in their approaches incrementally. For example, a fairly common transition for businesses is shifting from almost total reliance on traditional philanthropy (i.e., community sponsorships, grants to local nonprofits, employee volunteering, and fund-raising) to engaged philanthropy including multiyear partnerships with various community

---

[20] Tran, N. 2016. "A Portfolio Approach to Corporate Social Investment." *SVA Quarterly*, August 25, 2016. https://socialventures.com.au/sva-quarterly/a-portfolio-approach-to-corporate-social-investment/

[21] Id. (noting adaptation from M. Kramer, "Catalytic Philanthropy," *Stanford Social Innovation Review* (Fall 2009) and Porter, M., and M. Kramer. January–February 2011. "Creating Shared Value." *Harvard Business Review*.

organizations to address a large and important social issue such as supporting local schools and creating meaningful job opportunities for teen-
agers in the community who have grown up in difficult conditions.
As businesses become more involved in engaged philanthropy, often participating in multiple partnerships dealing with social issues that intersect
with their core businesses and resource competencies (e.g., Toyota formed
a community foundation to work with local nonprofit organizations on
projects relating to road safety, education, and the environment), they
may eventually decide to stretch for even greater impact through shared
value, such as launching a community innovation fund to combine financial and human capital to invent new technical solutions to social and
environmental issues.

Tran identified the first step toward developing a well-managed social
investment portfolio as defining the social and business objectives, and
the parameters, of the portfolio, a process that begins with figuring out
what impacts the business wants to have in carrying out its social investments. Businesses need to ask and answer several fundamental questions:
What does our society need? What does our business need? What are our
capabilities toward addressing the social issue? The next thing that needs
to be done is for the business to articulate the business-related motiva-
tions for its social investment activities, which might include, for example,
enhancing employee engagement, building customer loyalty, managing
downside risks to the company's reputation, contributing to business
innovation and growth opportunities, supporting community and causes,
engaging key stakeholders, and/or incubating shared value. Finally, the
business should think about the boundaries of its comfort zone for social
investing, which means considering how risk adverse the business is and
whether there are any causes and/or investment approaches that cause
discomfort or which are not aligned with the overall mission and strategy of the business. Available resources are an important consideration
at this point since each approach carries a different level of engagement
and responsibility (i.e., with traditional philanthropy the responsibility
for execution lies with the grantee, but catalytic philanthropy is based on
the business assuming responsibility and accountability).

Once the business has determined its social and business objectives,
the next step according to Tran is to use that information to assess the

alignment of each current and proposed social investment initiative against those objectives. A fairly simple way to do this is to score each initiative against the relevant criterion such as the social impact focus area, vision, strategy, core business skills, and resources. Once the scores have been computed each of the initiatives can be compared against the others to identify which ones are best aligned, and presumably worth continued support, and which ones may be poorly aligned and thus likely candidates for termination or de-emphasis. The idea is to prioritize initiatives to make the most efficient use of resources and create a social investment portfolio that includes initiatives that score well on both social and business value. In the process of developing the portfolio approach attention should be paid to creating processes that allow the business to track progress against projected impacts and make good decisions about changes in the portfolio as time goes by.

Traditional Philanthropy

The key issues associated with the practice of traditional philanthropy are which organizations and causes should the company support and how much should be contributed, with contributions mainly taking the form of cash with perhaps some employee volunteer efforts. In many cases, contributions are made for specific programs and/or equipment and in response to requests from community organizations or a particular crisis that adversely impacts the community. Traditional philanthropy programs often lack an underlying strategy, with decisions regarding donations being made on an ad hoc basis. Traditional philanthropy often extends to a large number of beneficiary organizations throughout the community; however, many grants are in relatively small amounts and are not awarded on a recurring basis.[22] A prototypical example of traditional corporate philanthropy is an organized campaign that solicits cash donations from employees, with matching contributions by the company, and a designated time during which employees provide volunteer services to the community organization that will be receiving the donations. Any assessment of the effectiveness and impact of donations made in a traditional corporate philanthropy

---

[22] Id.

program is generally informal and reporting typically is limited to a list of the organizations to which the company contributed.

Although many community nonprofit organizations still receive the bulk of their outside funding from governmental agencies and individual donors, funds from corporations, either directly or through corporate foundations, are obviously welcome and rigorously pursued during the course of nonprofit fund-raising efforts. Traditional corporate philanthropy has typically involved grants, matching gifts, in-kind contributions, partnering with local nonprofits, and volunteering resources from company employees. While companies, like individuals, are generally interested in making positive changes in their communities when engaging in philanthropy, they are also interested in other business-related benefits and opportunities from their actions including branding, product placement, and employee and community engagement.

While companies, particularly larger ones, seem to be making a shift from traditional philanthropy toward engaged philanthropy, shared value, and social investment, there is still room for charitable giving programs, particularly given the demonstrated positive impacts on employee engagement and commitment; however, companies need to rethink their approach to incorporate certain strategic principles. According to a survey of a number of corporate foundations conducted by the Boston Consulting Group (BCG), the following approaches are essential for a successful philanthropic program:[23]

- Companies need to set a clear mission and goals for their giving program and execute it with a clear understanding of what they are trying to achieve from both a business and social perspective. Companies should go through the process of developing a mission statement for their philanthropic program that clarifies why the company has chosen to support a particular cause, the purpose and goals of the program,

[23] Adapted from M. Silverstein, P. Chandran, and S. Cairns-Smith, "Rethinking Corporate Philanthropy" (Boston Consulting Group, May 9, 2013), https://bcg.com/publications/2013/corporate-social-responsibility-philanthropy-rethinking-corporate-philanthropy.aspx

what resources the company will provide, and what guidelines will be followed. The mission statement engages that choices about activities and causes that will be supported are made strategically rather than on an ad hoc basis as commonly done in the past.

- Companies should narrow the focus of the philanthropic programs and manage for impact. In the past, many companies diluted their efforts by managing a highly fragmented portfolio consisting of a number of small grants devoted to a wide range of causes. The sounder approach is to concentrate of a smaller number of causes, each of which is selected because they are aligned with the company's business and strategy and the verified interests of the company's main stakeholders. This often means eliminating, or substantially reducing, grants in non-core areas and making a smaller number, albeit usually larger, grants in the remaining target areas. Focus and concentration also allows the company to build expertise in a particular area and develop a reputation for leadership and participation with respect to the selected group of causes. In order to ensure that the selected programs are have the desired impact, provision must be made for rigorous measurement and monitoring of results.

- Companies need to improve their processes for identifying and selecting partners that are best equipped to achieve the program's goals and sustain its efforts beyond the period during which the company is providing its initial support. Partnerships should be made with nonprofit organizations that can assist with designing and executing the program and with other companies interested in the issue or activity that can bring complimentary skills and resources to the initiative. Care should be taken not to stretch resources too much by having too many partnerships and companies should seek to identify a small number of partners interested in long-term commitments, collaborating and communicating, and providing the company with recognition and visibility in the community.

- Technically grants made by corporate foundations should have no direct commercial benefit in order to maintain the nonprofit status of the foundation; however, decisions made regarding philanthropic giving, whether made directly by the company or through a corporate foundation, should be made following consultation with groups on the business side to obtain their input on what programs will be meet community needs and generate goodwill among the company's stakeholders. BCG provided several ideas about involving the business while maintaining legal compliance including holding annual "big ideas" forums with business leaders and key partners from the nonprofit world and nongovernmental organizations; involving business leaders in the grant evaluation process; or having business leaders act as champions for specific grants or giving areas.

- Companies often had difficulties deciding on the best way to communicate to stakeholders regarding the philanthropic programs; however, as interest in corporate social responsibility has increased, companies have been driven to create effective communications strategies that raise awareness of the social impact of the company's giving program and share the success of corporate-giving efforts in order to establish the company's commitment locally or globally. Employees, community members, and other stakeholders should receive regular reports on the company's philanthropy program and directors and executives should be kept informed so that they can include the program in their own internal and external communications regarding the business.

- Companies need to select the appropriate structure for their philanthropic programs and allocate resources and attention accordingly. In general, the choice comes down to funding the programs directly as a business expense or setting up a separate tax-exempt organization (i.e., a corporate foundation) to which funding is allocated solely for use on charitable purposes. Direct corporate giving provides the company with more flexibility; however, a foundation with prefunding from the company can

make multiyear investments, set and remain focused on specific
goals and objectives, and attract external talent that specializes
in managing philanthropy. A foundation facilitates the strategic focus mentioned above; however, there are overhead costs
associated with a foundation and care must be taken to ensure
that the activities of the foundation are aligned with the needs
of business, taking into account the need to comply with legal
guidelines. Many companies use a combination of direct giving
for small grants, perhaps one-time sponsorships of events
recommended by employees, and a corporate foundation.

Making the business case for corporate philanthropy has been complicated by the challenges of demonstrating a direct link between philanthropy and financial performance due to the lack of objective measures
of philanthropy and the social impact of philanthropy; disagreements
regarding how to measure corporate financial performance; the long pay-
back periods associated with many philanthropic projects and initiatives;
and the reluctance of companies to make full disclosures of their philanthropic investments and activities. Further complicating the situation is
the diversity in the areas upon which corporate philanthropic programs
have focused including public health, nutrition, and welfare; educational
and employment opportunities; the development of a stronger climate for
doing business; environmental impacts; and international/disaster relief.[24]

Engaged Philanthropy

Engaged philanthropy involves a wider range of resources than traditional
philanthropy, although the total value of the resources invested may not
be much more than the contributions that the company makes through
traditional philanthropy. Engaged philanthropy uses money, time, information, networks, skills, goods and services, and influence to support a
small group of community partners to deliver a discernable social impact
(e.g., building the capacity of community organizations involved working

---

[24] *The Business Case for Corporate Philanthropy* (L. W. Seidman Research Institute,
Arizona State University, November 2015), iii.

on a social or environmental cause). Engaged philanthropy focuses on identifying a relatively small number of recipients and forging strategic alliances that will typically extend for several years and involve larger grants. Engaged philanthropy is used to make an impact on specific targeted areas or issues that should be aligned with the company's mission and specific goals and objectives for community involvement. Contributions that are an extension of the company's core competencies is a hallmark of engaged philanthropy.[25]

Engaged philanthropy has been described as incorporating social impact management into a company's philanthropy program to create long-term value, and engaged philanthropic programs include the following elements:[26]

- Investment in the community, with a view to adding capacity to a certain field or building that field from the ground up, a view that requires a long-term commitment
- Alignment of grants with business strategy and utilizing a range of cash and non-cash resources to support organizations or issues that generate social impact in an area that provides long-term value to the business as well as society
- Development of a "signature program" to focus corporate resources and extend impact over the long term
- Nurturing of strong relationships with grantee organizations (e.g., by having members of the senior management team serve on the board of directors of community organizations), community leaders, and other stakeholders
- Conducting rigorous impact measurement (including interim evaluation metrics) that attempts to understand the long-term term effects of funding on the societal changes the grant seeks to achieve.

---

[25] Tran, N. 2016. "A Portfolio Approach to Corporate Social Investment." *SVA Quarterly*, August 25, 2016. https://socialventures.com.au/sva-quarterly/a-portfolio-approach-to-corporate-social-investment/
[26] Parkinson, A. May 2016. *Using Corporate Philanthropy to Build Long-Term Perspectives*, 6. The Conference Board, Giving Thoughts.

According to the Aspen Institute, "social impact management" considers and evaluates three aspects of a business: the purpose—in both societal and business terms—of a business or business activity; social context, including whether the legitimate rights and responsibilities of multiple stakeholders are considered and whether a proposed strategy is being evaluated in terms that include not only predicted business outcomes but also broader impacts on the quality of life, the wider economy of a region and security and safety; and measurement of performance and profitability across both short- and long-term time frames.[27] Social impact management can be applied to every traditional business topic, from accounting to marketing to strategy;[28] however, integration may be difficult, particularly the shift toward focusing on long-term value, and this makes a company's philanthropic program a good vehicle for shifting company thinking. Engaged philanthropy also addresses the growing interest of institutional investors in demonstrated social responsibility by their portfolio companies and the need for companies to proactively manage the expectations of key stakeholders such as individuals and groups in the communities in which the companies operate.

Catalytic Philanthropy

Kramer argued that even though traditional American philanthropists had spent vast amounts of money and helped to create the world's largest

---

[27] Id. at 3 (citing "Social Impact Management: A Definition." The Aspen Institute).

[28] Business topics and disciplines and their associated social impact management topics include accounting (full cost accounting and social auditing); finance (discussion of social venture capital and social investing); information technology (digital divide, social impacts of technology transfer, and workforce impact of IT enhancements); marketing (social and cause-related marketing and cultural impacts of advertising messages); operations management (plant siting decisions and stakeholders, risk management, impacts of labor standards); organizational behavior (employee rights and participation, workplace equity and diversity issues) and strategy (corporate reputation/image, downsizing, operating in economically disadvantaged areas and corporate governance). Id. at 5 (citing "Social Impact Management: A Definition," The Aspen Institute).

nonprofit sector, they had fallen far short in their efforts to solve the country's most pressing problems.[29] He noted that while annual charitable giving in the United States had grown by 255 percent between 1980 and 2005, and the number of nonprofits in the United States had more than doubled to 1.3 million during that same period, the U.S. position among the members of the Organisation for Economic Co-Operation and Development in basic measures of health, education, and economic opportunity had dropped from second to 12th. While conceding that larger political and economic forces play a much larger role in the persistence of childhood poverty and failed schools, Kramer called on donors to adopt a new approach to social change, which he described as "catalytic philanthropy."

Tran identified the following key question with respect to catalytic philanthropy: "How can we catalyze a campaign that achieves a measurable social impact?" Catalytic philanthropy brings to be bear new and different resources in additional to those deployed in engaged philanthropy, notably the experience and expertise that companies should be able to provide in the areas of leadership and coordination, research and knowledge, networks, and new business models. Catalytic philanthropy typically focuses on a single systematic issue with the goal of establishing a leader and catalyst for change. The unique expertise found in the for-profit business world is applied to forging and managing cross-sector collaboration that involves multiple partners focused on that single issue.[30] Relying on a decade of work as a social impact advisor to innovative donors, Kramer identified four distinctive practices that contributed to the effectiveness of catalytic philanthropists:

They have the ambition to change the world and the courage to accept responsibility for achieving the results they seek; they engage others in a compelling campaign, empowering stakeholders and creating the conditions for collaboration and innovation;

[29] Kramer, M. Fall 2009. "Catalytic Philanthropy." *Stanford Social Innovation Review*, https://ssir.org/articles/entry/catalytic_philanthropy

[30] Tran, N. 2016. "A Portfolio Approach to Corporate Social Investment." *SVA Quarterly*, August 25, 2016. https://socialventures.com.au/sva-quarterly/a-portfolio-approach-to-corporate-social-investment/

they use all of the tools that are available to create change, including unconventional ones from outside the nonprofit sector; and they create actionable knowledge to improve their own effectiveness and to influence the behavior of others.[31]

As background for Kramer's arguments and illustrations of the practices of catalytic philanthropy, it is important to understand some of the practical limitations of traditional philanthropy (i.e., the main action by donors is deciding which nonprofits to support and how much and what to give them, leaving responsibility for finding and implementing solutions to social problems fully in the hands of the nonprofit), which remains valuable in certain instances. Kramer does not question the good intentions of those working in the nonprofit sector; however, he notes that it is important to understand that most nonprofits are very small and operate with limited budgets that severely restrict the resources that any one nonprofit can bring to a particular problem. In addition, while there are efforts to build networks among nonprofits in most cases any one organization will be operating largely on its own without ready access to sources of best practices and the collective clout to influence governmental actions. In fact, collaboration among nonprofits is often difficult because they are continuously competing with one another to convince donors that their solution and approach to a particular issue is better than other nonprofits with a similar focus. Most nonprofits also fail to measure and publicize the impact of their activities, which impedes their own planning and makes fund-raising more challenging. All of these limitations taken together create a nonprofit sector that often cannot scale its activities and resources to the point where it can provide meaningful and sustainable assistance to the many people needing the services that nonprofits can render.

The first practice of catalytic philanthropy—taking responsibility for achieving results—begins with donors selecting an issue of great personal significance to them that has raised a sense of urgency and commitment such that they want to take an active role in addressing the problem beyond the traditional path of simply making passive donations to nonprofits and

---

[31] Id. The discussion of the four practices of catalytic philanthropy in this section is adapted from his cited article.

other community groups. Hallmarks of this practice include becoming deeply knowledgeable about the issue; actively recruiting collaborators and often creating a new separate entity (e.g., a foundation) specifically dedicated to the particular issue or cause; formulating clear and practical goals and identifying the steps that need to be taken in order to achieve those goals; leveraging personal and professional relationships; creating new business models after the extensive research on the particular issue; coordinating the activities of different nonprofits; and proactively influencing governmental actions and public awareness of the issue. Behind all of this is the ability and will to bring connections, capacity, and clout that most nonprofits do not have to finding solutions to a problem. However, this does not mean trying to act alone, imposing a solution that has not been vetted by the intended beneficiaries or ignoring the value that nonprofits, community groups, and other stakeholders can bring to developing and implementing a collective solution.

The second practice of catalytic philanthropy is a concerted effort by the donor to go beyond individual grants to mobilize an entire campaign to influence change with respect to a specific issue or problem. Mobilization efforts often focus on breaking down bottlenecks and institutional impediments to change by forging cross-sector collaborations and mobilizing multiple stakeholders to create shared solutions. Some issues cry out for this type of approach: improving educational success and outcomes calls for action across the entire continuum of student progress and can only be done effectively if the initiative engages school districts, teacher groups, universities, private and corporate donors, governmental representatives, and community groups. Change campaigns of this type heighten awareness and bring badly needed coordination to solving complex problems; however, they require patience to work slowly and carefully bring more and more stakeholders to the table and convince them to set aside some of their individual concerns to contribute to the larger effort that will have the greatest impact.

The third practice of catalytic philanthropy, using all available tools, captures the observation that more and more donors are going beyond traditional grant making to introduce a wide variety of tools to promote social change that they are used to working with in situations throughout the for-profit aspects of their activities. As examples Kramer pointed to contribution of corporate resources (e.g., supporting efforts to improve math and science education by having the corporation and its employees provide technology, management advice and intensive tutoring, mentoring, summer employment opportunities, and scholarships); investment capital, such as subordinated debt to strengthen the balance of sheet of a local community development corporation; advocacy and litigation; lobbying and using capital and contacts to implement sophisticated communications strategies that are more impactful than traditional low budget public service announcements.

The last of the four practices of catalytic philanthropy was described by Kramer as the creation of "actionable knowledge," which refers to proactive collection and analysis of relevant information about an issue or problem by the donors (as opposed to relying on nonprofits to provide the information so that donor can decide whether to make a passive grant) and use of that information to make decisions about how they will act and motive the actions of others. For example, when taking action on a problem such as improving primary and secondary education in local schools, a donor may organize and distribute data regarding school performance throughout the community so that community members can use the data to create solutions for specific schools and identify the schools that might be a good source for mining best practices. When knowledge is organized and presented in a dramatic fashion, perhaps through short documentary videos, stakeholders can be simultaneously entertained, informed, and engaged.

Kramer acknowledged that catalytic philanthropy is not appropriate for all donors, most of whom simply do not have the time or resources to do more than engage in traditional philanthropy and do the best they can to select appropriate and effective nonprofits. Catalytic philanthropy is difficult because best practices for the approach are still developing and engaging in catalytic philanthropy requires a significant change in the mindset of companies and their foundations to transition from being donors to agents for change. Among other things catalytic philanthropy calls for new skills and a re-thinking of the culture and self-perception of the company and/or its foundation. Finally, the success of catalytic philanthropy depends on the willingness of the beneficiaries and others already involved in the specific cause or issue (i.e., governmental agencies) to embrace the leadership and coordination skills offered by the company or foundation.

Creating Shared Value

While "creating shared value" is discussed as an extension of philanthropic approaches, it is somewhat unique in that it is essentially grounded in business strategy with the goal of addressing social problems at the same time that the company continues to pursue its traditional mission of creating economic benefit. As discussed below, creating shared value asks companies, investors, and other stakeholders to accept that using the resources of a business to solve social problems is not inconsistent with growing the business and advancing the company's competitive advantage. Creating shared value is based on the assumption that business objectives can be aligned with creation of value for customers, community members, and suppliers. Rather than focusing primarily on the systematic changes associated with catalytic philanthropy, creating social value allows companies to do what they do best: develop new products and more sustainable processes through cross-sector partnerships and collaborations.[32]

Spitzeck and Chapman explained that the concept of shared value dates back to the 1980s to the definition of corporate culture, which incorporated the notion of shared values as being clearly articulated organizational values that make a significant difference in the lives of employees, as well as in the organization's performance.[33] Shared values were seen as an important way to align employees with the objective and purpose of the business. The idea of alignment was subsequently applied to other business relationships and transactions including the supply chain and customers. The 1980s and 1990s also saw the application of shared values to interactions between business and society including actions taken with respect to local development. Spitzeck and Chapman believed that it was important to understand that Porter and Kramer's arguments and recommendations with respect to shared value, while innovative, were nonetheless grounded in an extensive body of previous research relating to

[32] Tran, N. 2016. "A Portfolio Approach to Corporate Social Investment." *SVA Quarterly*, August 25, 2016. https://socialventures.com.au/sva-quarterly/a-port-folio-approach-to-corporate-social-investment/

[33] Spitzeck, H., and S. Chapman. 2012. "Creating Shared Value as a Differentiation Strategy—The Example of BASF in Brazil." *Corporate Governance* 12, no. 4, 499–500.

bottom-of-the-pyramid markets, sustainable supply chains and industry clusters for local development.[34]

Porter and Kramer have been strident advocates of businesses making a fundamental shift in their purposes away from short-term financial performance toward coming together with the society in which they operate to create "shared value": "creating economic value in a way that also creates value for society by addressing its needs and challenges."[35] Porter argued that only businesses can create prosperity; however, companies, particularly in the aftermath of the financial crisis of the late 2000s, are often perceived as prospering at the expense of the broader community and, in many cases, have been viewed as being a major cause of social, environmental, and economic problems.[36] The response to the actual and alleged issues associated with business activities has often been hostile to companies, with government and civil society often taking steps that companies see as harmful to their efforts to create stakeholder value. Porter noted that while businesses have concentrated more on corporate social responsibility overall perceptions of the legitimacy of the business was declining.

Porter believed that mounting concern regarding environmental and social issues could only be addressed by a new evolution of capitalism in which businesses continued their traditional pursuit of economic value by creating societal value (i.e., shared value). Porter and Kramer defined shared value as follows:

> The concept of shared value can be defined as policies and operating practices that enhance competitiveness of a company while simultaneously advancing the economic and social conditions in the communities in which it operates. . . . Value is defined as benefits relative to costs, not just benefits alone.[37]

---

[34] Id.

[35] Porter, M., and M. Kramer. January–February 2011. "Creating Shared Value." *Harvard Business Review*, 64.

[36] Porter, M. 2011. *Creating Shared Value: Redefining Capitalism and the Role of the Corporation in Society*, 2. Slide Deck Presentation at FSG CSV Leadership Summit.

[37] Porter, M. and M. Kramer. January–February 2011. "Creating Shared Value." *Harvard Business Review*, 66.

It is important to note that Porter and Kramer were not asking businesses to set aside their drive to achieve profitability; however, as Porter
pointed out, all profit is not equal and turning their focus toward profit
involving shared value will cause society to advance more quickly while
allowing companies to grow faster.[38]

Spitzeck and Chapman noted that while Porter and Kramer's approach
was consistent with prior applications of shared values to the relationship
between business and society, it also introduced two new conditions: shared
value strategies must create value for the company by enhancing competitiveness and must create value for society by advancing social conditions
in the communities in which the company operates.[39] Spitzeck and Chapman also pointed out that by providing that societal value is defined relative to costs Porter and Kramer were embracing a strategic philanthropy
approach, which is concerned with the efficiency and effectiveness of social
outcomes relative to investments (i.e., getting the most social impact per
dollar spent).[40] The key question here is how to have more societal impact
per dollar spent. Porter and Kramer's concern for performance was further
highlighted by their insistence that shared value strategies "be data driven,
clearly linked to defined outcomes, well connected to the goals of all stakeholders, and tracked with clear metrics."[41]

Porter noted that shared value would require a major transformation
in management thinking to incorporate societal issues into strategy and
operations.[42] According to Porter and Kramer, shared value can be pursued

---

[38] Porter, M. 2011. "Creating Shared Value: Redefining Capitalism and the Role
of the Corporation in Society." (Slide Deck Presentation at FSG CSV Leadership
Summit, June 9, 2011), 3. Porter explained that creating share value was not
philanthropy, "giving back" harm reduction, (just) sustainability, triple bottom
line, or balancing stakeholder interests. Id. at 4.

[39] Spitzeck, H., and S. Chapman. 2012. "Creating Shared Value As a Differentiation Strategy—The Example of BASF in Brazil." *Corporate Governance* 12, no. 4,
499, 500–501.

[40] Id.

[41] Porter, M., and M. Kramer. January–February 2011. "Creating Shared Value."
Harvard Business Review, 76.

[42] Porter, M. June 9, 2011. *Creating Shared Value: Redefining Capitalism and the Role of
the Corporation in Society*, 3. Slide Deck Presentation at FSG CSV Leadership Summit.

and created by businesses in three distinct ways: by reconceiving products and services to address societal needs and/or by opening new markets by redesigning products or adopting different distribution methods in order to serve unmet needs in underserved communities; redefining productivity in the value chain; and building strong and supportive industry clusters with capable local suppliers and institutions and a healthy business environment in the communities in which the company operates.[43]

Focusing on products, services, and markets allows businesses to contribute in ways in which they are simply more effective and experience than governments and nongovernmental organizations. By integrating shared value into their strategies, companies can take advantage of new opportunities for innovation, differentiation, and growth. Sometimes the change in mindset is difficult for established firms and it is not surprising to see that sustainable entrepreneurs often take the lead in identifying and capturing shared value opportunities.[44] Spitzeck and Chapman noted that the approach of reconceiving products and markets had previously been introduced and discussed as *Business at the Bottom of the Pyramid* by Prahalad and Hart in the early 2000s and explained their belief that the basic argument in support of the approach was creating economies of scale for offering essential products and services such as health, housing, or credit at reasonable prices to disadvantaged communities, thus fostering their inclusion within the formal economy.[45] For Porter and Kramer the idea was that businesses should focus their product- and market-related competencies and strategies on "satisfying unmet social needs" and "serving disadvantaged communities."[46]

---

[43] Porter, M., and M. Kramer. January–February 2011. "Creating Shared Value." *Harvard Business Review*, 67.

[44] Porter, M. June 9, 2011. "Creating Shared Value: Redefining Capitalism and the Role of the Corporation in Society." Slide Deck Presentation at FSG CSV Leadership Summit, 6.

[45] Spitzeck, H., and S. Chapman. 2012. "Creating Shared Value as a Differentiation Strategy—The Example of BASF in Brazil." *Corporate Governance* 12, no. 4, 499–501.

[46] Porter, M., and M. Kramer. January–February 2011. "Creating Shared Value." *Harvard Business Review*, 67–68.

One challenge for businesses is selecting the social need they wish to address through their shared value strategies and operations. Porter noted that products and services can be designed with a focus on environmental impact, safety, health, education, nutrition, living with disability, housing, financial security, and much more. As for the broader question of identifying product and market opportunities to create shared value, Porter recommended that companies redefine their businesses around unsolved customer problems or concerns as opposed to traditional product definitions; think in terms of improving lives and not just meeting consumer needs; identify customer groups that have been poorly served or overlooked by the industry's products in both advanced and emerging markets; and start the process with no preconceived constraints about product attributes, channel configuration, or the economic model of the business.[47]

As for Porter and Kramer's recommendation that businesses redefine productivity in the value chain, Spitzeck and Chapman noted that their approach consisted of a holistic evaluation of value chain that included firm infrastructure (e.g., financing, planning, investor relations); human resource management (e.g., recruiting, training, compensation system); technology development (e.g., product design, testing, process design, material research, and market research); procurement; in-bound logistics; operations; outbound logistics; marketing and sales; and after-sales service.[48] Porter and Kramer argued that businesses can apply shared value to identify opportunities for improvement in key areas such as procurement, resource use, energy use, logistical efficiency, employee productivity, and the location of facilities and the supply chain while simultaneously improving

---

[47] Porter, M. June 9, 2011. "Creating Shared Value: Redefining Capitalism and the Role of the Corporation in Society." Slide Deck Presentation at FSG CSV Leadership Summit, 6 and 9.

[48] Spitzeck, H., and S. Chapman. 2012. "Creating Shared Value as a Differentiation Strategy—The Example of BASF in Brazil." *Corporate Governance* 12, no. 4, 499, 501–502; and Porter, M. June 9, 2011. "Creating Shared Value: Redefining Capitalism and the Role of the Corporation in Society." Slide Deck Presentation at FSG CSV Leadership Summit, 10.

economic, environmental, and social conditions in the communities where the company is operating. A few of the opportunities throughout the value chain mentioned by Porter for a company engaged in the mining sector included:[49]

- *Human Resource Management*: Recruiting from disadvantaged communities; diversity; employee education and job training; safe working conditions; onsite housing so that miners can be closer to their families; employee health; compensation and benefits to support low-income workers; and staff retaining and rehabilitation after a mine closes
- *Mine Acquisition, Development, and Operations*: Energy and water use; worker safety and labor practices; limiting emissions and waste; biodiversity and low ecological impacts; minimizing effects of hazardous materials; recovering additional materials from "exhausted" mines; and minimizing outbound logistical impacts
- *Technology Development*: Enhancing partnerships with colleges and universities

One example of the shared value approach in action with respect to the value chain is the efforts of Nestle to redesign its coffee procurement processes. Nestle targeted smaller farms in impoverished areas that were suffering due to low productivity, poor quality, and environmental degradation and set out to provide support to those farms through advice on farming practices; assistance in securing plant stock, fertilizers, and pesticides; and directly paying them a premium for better quality beans. The results created substantial value for both parties and the environment: farmers' incomes went up due to the higher yields and improved quality of their beans, Nestle enjoyed a more stable and reliable supply of good

---

[49] Porter, M. June 9, 2011. "Creating Shared Value: Redefining Capitalism and the Role of the Corporation in Society." Slide Deck Presentation at FSG CSV Leadership Summit, 11.

coffee and the adverse environmental impact of the farming activities declined in a manner that was sustainable.[50]

Porter and Kramer's recommendation that businesses create clusters for local development follows from previous research that demonstrated that industry clusters enhance innovation, competitiveness, and knowledge exchange; shared values align the activities of the actors within clusters; and collaboration and knowledge exchange on sustainability issues in clusters improves environmental and social performance.[51] Spitzeck and Chapman noted that the insights from clustering research were also being applied to local development contexts, which similarly depend on the interaction and alignment of several players such as suppliers, service providers, educational institutions, NGOs, and local governments in order to attain to local development goals.[52]

Porter's arguments for clustering was based on several compelling business propositions: strong local clusters improved company productivity due to greater supply chain efficiency, lower environmental impact, and better access to skills; companies, working collaboratively to build local clusters, could catalyze major improvements in the cluster and the local business environment; and developing local clusters strengthens linkages between company and community success (i.e., what's good for the company is good for the community).[53] He recommended that businesses look to see what suppliers are inefficiency or missing locally and what institutional weaknesses or community deficits are creating internal costs for the firm. The answers to these questions provide the ideas for development-based clustering activities, such as launching education and training programs to

---

[50] The discussion in this paragraph is adapted from an executive summary of Porter, M., and M. Kramer. January–February 2011. "Creating Shared Value." *Harvard Business Review*.

[51] Spitzeck, H., and S. Chapman. 2012. "Creating Shared Value as a Differentiation Strategy—The Example of BASF in Brazil." *Corporate Governance* 12, no. 4, 499–502.

[52] Id.

[53] Porter, M. June 9, 2011. "Creating Shared Value: Redefining Capitalism and the Role of the Corporation in Society." Slide Deck Presentation at FSG CSV Leadership Summit, 13.

be sure that there is a sufficient pool of skilled labor in each of the communities where the company operates and creating an investment fund to support a network of small- and medium-sized businesses that can fill gaps in the supply chain and provide the company with improved services and quality while creating a large number of new jobs in the community.[54]

Porter made it clear that the shared value approach was not the same as corporate social responsibility (CSR) and that even some of the firms that had been recognized for their CSR efforts would need to do more in order to truly and effectively transition to shared value. For both CSR and shared value it is assumed that companies are committed to complying with laws and ethical standards and acting in ways that reduce environmental and social harm. Key distinctions, however, are as follows: while CSR is based on "doing good" by acting as a good citizen and engaging in philanthropy, shared value has a sharper focus on value creating for the community and the company, with detailed measurement of value taking into account economic and societal benefits relative to cost; CSR is discretionary, although it is expected more and more by important stakeholders such as investors, while shared value is essential to profit maximization and competing effectively; CSR agendas are often determined externally while shared value priorities and initiatives should be driven by the needs and competencies of the particular business; and the impact of CSR is limited by the corporate footprint and CSR budget while shared value mobilizes the entire corporate budget.[55] Porter counseled businesses to act as businesses, not as charitable givers, and argued that in doing so businesses can achieve renewed purpose and be perceived as legitimate and valued contributors to the well-being of their communities.

Porter and Kramer are obviously not the only proponents of shared value and other consultants have praised the concept and offered additional ideas about how businesses might proceed such as sustainable social investments. Social investments have been described as "repayable finance that aims to achieve a social and financial return" and provide businesses with a path for engaging deeply in social causes while realizing strategic opportunities to learn about new markets, growing an existing market,

[54] Id. at 14 and 15.
[55] Id. at 16.

foster innovation, and generate sustainable financial returns.[56] Research conducted in 2016 covering 557 corporate social impact programs at 127 companies around the world showed that the most common vehicles used to generate financial returns are targeted at commercial development, infrastructure development, product development, or social supply chains.[57] As for the more frequently used approaches to funding and social investments, the preferences were corporate social funds that combine regular financial performance with stated social impact goals; social impact bonds, an investment vehicle whose payoff is dependent on a specific social outcome such as expanding the reach and impact of a particular community development program; corporate venture capital that focuses on significant investments in, and acquisitions of, firms with a social impact that align with the company's core business; social joint ventures and social business units that can be used to pursue long-term business goals (e.g., investigating new markets and/or developing new products and business models) in a manner more closely tied to core business operations without have to purchase new businesses.[58]

Social investments, like all of the shared value approaches, require attention from the leaders of the organization and special efforts to overcome barriers such as a lack of awareness of social investment models and a cultural mindset to concentration on traditional philanthropy. One consultant recommended that companies looking to launch a social investment program need to raise awareness of social investment opportunities within the firm; educate stakeholders about the benefits that social investment can bring across the business; establish dedicated representatives to review how longer-term social initiatives could benefit the business; ensure that the company has access to tools that will effectively measure social returns; and engage with other companies, intermediaries, and advisors who can highlight opportunities and mechanisms for launching social investment programs. Companies should start small and

---

[56] *Corporate Social Investment: Gaining Traction* (Oliver Wyman, 2016).

[57] Id. at 4.

[58] Id. at 4–6. For case studies of various shared value initiatives, see *Exploring Shared Value in Global Health and Safety* (National Academies Press, 2016), https://nap.edu/read/23501/chapter/5

once there is a track record to support scaling up they can implement more sophisticated approaches such as long-term partnerships, joint ventures, and social business units. Networking also plays an important role since social investment is often most effective when done in collaboration with like-minded organizations.[59]

Smart Partnering

According to Keys et al., CSR encompasses dual objectives: pursuing benefits for the business and for society.[60] They used these two objectives to create a map of the CSR landscape using two dimensions: benefit to society and benefit to business and then populated that map with four popular activities that have generally been included under the umbrella of CSR. For example, "pet projects," activities selected by individual executives based on their personal interests, are often supported by companies, yet generally have little benefit to either society or the business. Philanthropy is another common CSR approach and generally does well in terms of benefit to society; however, unless philanthropy is done strategically it can be subject to criticism as providing little in the way of benefit to the business of the company. Some companies engage in what have been derogatively termed "propaganda" activities that are primarily intended to enhance the company's reputation but do not produce much in the way of social benefit and often put the company at risk for criticism if it appears that its actions are not as strong as its words. Finally, partnering appears on the map as providing significant benefits on both the societal and business dimensions.

Keys et al. argued that "smart partnering" was an effective way for companies to create value for both the business and society simultaneously by leveraging the complementary capabilities of both partners to develop creative solutions to address major challenges that affect each partner.[61] Keys et al. explained that with partnering the focus of the business moved

---

[59] *Corporate Social Investment: Gaining Traction* (Oliver Wyman, 2016), 8–9.

[60] Keys, T., T. Malnight, and K. van der Graaf. December 2009. "Making the Most of Corporate Social Responsibility." *McKinsey Quarterly*,

[61] Id.

beyond avoiding risks or enhancing reputation and toward improving the company's core value creation abilities and addressing long-term challenges to the company's sustainability. As for society, the focus of partnering extends beyond maintenance of minimum standards or seeking funding to make an impact on important social issues such as improving employment, overall quality of life and living standards.

Keys et al. urged company leaders to map all of the current and proposed CSR initiatives and activities based on the two dimensions described above. Mapping allows leaders to get a better idea of where the company's CSR activities have been focused in the past and where they should be focused in the future. When completing the mapping exercise, leaders should pay particular attention to identifying the objectives of each activity; the benefits that are being created by each activity, including who is actually realizing those benefits; and how relevant the activity is to addressing key strategic challenges and opportunities of the company. Answering these questions is important because every company, regardless of its size, has resource limitations that will apply to CSR initiatives. In addition, a "deep dive" mapping exercise will force the company to develop and use rigorous measurement and assessment tools in order to develop a clear picture of the impact of its CSR activities, tools that can be put to good use when the company establishes the framework for partnering activities.

Once the mapping process is completed, the information should be used to generate ideas for maximizing both the business and social benefits of the company's CSR activities. Keys et al. argued that this meant moving away from the relatively easy CSR activities that companies generally embrace because they are easier to execute—pet projects, philanthropy, and propaganda—toward partnering. Companies were advised to concentrate their CSR efforts, making sure that limited time and resources were focused on high business and social impact projects; build a deep understanding of both the business and social objectives and benefits of prospective projects; and find the right partners, partners who offer complementary strengths and have the motivation, and provide the requisite chemistry, to forge long-term sustainable relationships. Partnering activities, much like potential CSR topics, are abundant and each company needs to be smart in their selection process and ask additional questions such as what are the one or two criteria areas in its business where it inter-faces and has an impact on society and also has significant opportunities for enhancing the value of the business; what are the core long-term needs for the company and society that can be addressed through a particular partnership; and what resources or capabilities are needed in order for the partnership to be successful and which of these can the company offer through its existing core competencies and innovation capabilities.

Keys et al. emphasized the CSR partnering arrangements are like any other business relationship in that they need to be grounded in a solid business case and approached with rigor as to prioritization, planning, resourcing, and monitoring. The premise behind "smart partnering" for CSR is that it will deliver short-term and long-term benefits to busi-nesses and communities; however, those benefits need to be identified and defined in advance so that internal and external stakeholders, includ-ing shareholders, can be presented with a feasible story that elicits their support for the arrangement and the investment of resources that will be required from the company. Keys et al. suggested that the benefits associ-ated with a prospective partnering arrangement could be assessed across three dimensions:

- *Time Frame:* The time frame is important for CSR partner-ships, particularly since the initiatives are typically complex and thus require a longer period of time in order to fully real-ize their potential. The business case needs to be clear about both short-term immediate objectives for the partnership and longer-term benefits.
- *Nature of Benefits:* CSR partnerships generate both tangible and intangible benefits, both of which need to be measured in some way and taken into account. Companies are certainly interested in increasing revenues from gaining access to new markets and this can be easily tracked; however, notice and recognition need to be given to important intangible benefits such as development of new capabilities and enhancement of employee morale.
- *Benefit Split:* Smart partnering is based on generating benefits that are shared between business and society and in order for

the business case for the partnership to be effective it needs to be demonstrated that both business and society will benefit and that the allocation will be appropriate and not one-sided (if they are one-sided what has been touted as a partnership may really be philanthropy or propaganda).

For both businesses and society, consideration needs to be given to short- and long-term tangible benefits and short- and long-term intangible benefits. While each prospective partnership should be evaluated based on the three dimensions described above, it is not strictly necessary that each of them measure the same way on each of the dimensions; however, each arrangement should fit well into the company's overall portfolio of CSR partnerships and meet the minimum criteria for partnership status (i.e., there should be both short- and long-term benefits and benefits should not be extremely one-sided). Keys et al. illustrated the application of the three-dimension evaluation framework, and the room for different yet complimentary types of projects, by considering two partnerships that Unilever embarked on in the late 2000s: Project Shakti, which provided short-term tangible benefits that were extremely clear and powerful, and Project Kericho, which was undertaken to pursue and achieve long-term intangible benefits that were strategically critical for both the business and the communities in which the company was operating.

Project Shakti began as an initiative to financially empower rural women and create livelihood opportunities, including a regular income stream, for them and their families while, at the same time, providing a means for Hindustan Unilever (HUL) to market and sell its health and beauty care products to low-income consumers in rural Indian villages that often lie entirely outside the reach of mainstream media and cannot be reached cost effectively through the usual marketing channels. In order to reach consumers in these villages, HUL recruited local female entrepreneurs, referred to as Shakti Ammas ("Shakti" for power and "Amma" for mother), across 15 states to act as salespeople and brand-builders, and HUL's products were delivered to central locations where Shakti Ammas purchased the goods and from there to thousands of villages.

From a business perspective, Project Shakti created both short-term tangible benefits in the form of significant sales growth and long-term tangible benefits through HUL's ability to scale a cost-efficient distribution and sales network in remote markets. Intangible benefits to HUL included corporate reputation, education, and enhancement of brand loyalty. As for social benefits, HUL trained and employed thousands of women in villages across India in business basics and distribution management and substantially improved health and living standards (i.e., tangible benefits). Intangible social benefits from the program included the development of entrepreneurial skills and mindset and support for rural entrepreneurship.[62] It should be noted that in many cases the benefits identified for society will lead to subsequent opportunities for the business. For example, development of a community of entrepreneurs will hopefully lead to future partnerships with local firms to develop products that meet community needs and that will be enticing for consumers in those communities eager to support the efforts of their neighbors.

The Kericho Project took place in the Kericho district of southwestern Kenya where Unilever had been growing tea since 1924. At its Kericho estate, which is Rainforest Alliance certified, Unilever made a decision to provide workers with pay and working conditions significantly above the agricultural workers' norm and minimum statutory requirements and also offered housing, annual leave pay, transport allowances, paternity and maternity leave, free health care, nursery and primary school education, clean potable drinking water, and free meals during working hours.[63] In addition, Unilever entered into a partnership with the Sustainable Trade Initiative

---

[62] See Hindustan Unilever Limited, https://hul.co.in/sustainable-living/case-studies/enhancing-livelihoods-through-project-shakti.html; and Narsalay, R., R. Coffey and A. Sen. 2012. "Hindustan Unilever: Scaling a Cost-Efficient Distribution and Sales Network in Remote Markets." *Accenture Institute for High Performance*, https://accenture.com/_acnmedia/Accenture/Conversion-Assets/DotCom/Documents/Global/PDF/Dualpub_23/Accenture-Unilever-Case-Study.pdf

[63] Unilever's operation of the tea estates in Kericho became a significant challenge for the company in 2013 following allegations of sexual harassment of female workers and Unilever accepted and implemented accepted recommendations to improve the gender balance among team leaders and the grievance handling system following an extensive independent review of the allegations. See https://unilever.com/sustainable-living/what-matters-to-you/kericho-tea-estates.html

and the Kenya Tea Development Agency that has provided training to over 85,000 farmers on sustainable agricultural practices and Rainforest Alliance certification through Farmer Field Schools, including over 45,000 women (53 percent), and which has resulted in income diversification, higher yields and health, food and nutrition improvements.[64] Short-term tangible business benefits to Unilever included a positive impact on sales in selected countries and long-term tangible business benefits included control of critical raw material supplies and increased brand strength. Unilever also realized intangible business benefits such as an engaged, healthy workforce, corporate reputation, and eco-friendly brands. The local farmers and their communities benefited from increased income, resource and environmental protection, improved skills and entrepreneurial knowledge, improved living standards, and exposure to role models for economic development.

Keys et al. explained that the process of using the framework to identify, quantify, and categories the benefits available through a potential partnership not only allowed the company to develop the business case for the project, it also provided the foundation for communicating the story behind and rationale for the project to stakeholders. In order to communicate and report properly and fully, the company must have a clear understanding of the benefits to the business and society and the resources, including time, which will need to be invested in achieving those benefits. At the same time, the company and each prospective partner must have an understanding of the strategic challenges they are attempting to overcome and the resources they can offer through the partnership to collaborate effectively to address those challenges. Keys et al. counseled the companies looking to make smart partnering a strategic imperative and an opportunity needed to focus on key areas of interaction between the company and its environment and address value creation activities at the center of the company's strategic agenda. In addition, companies needed to look beyond the traditional comfort zones of pet projects and philanthropy and stretch their strategic ambitions for CSR to include smart partnering. Companies should also embrace smart partnering as a vehicle for demonstrating and executing on their core values.

---

[64] https://idhsustainabletrade.com/news/sustainable-agricultural-programme-ktda-idh-unilever-improves-livelihood-tea-farmers/

In order to get started on the journey toward smart partnering for sustainability, Keys et al. recommended that company leaders identify two or three critical interactions between the company's business and society and for each of these interactions map out what the company has to offer in terms of capabilities, knowledge, resources, and relationships that would contribute to overcoming both business and societal challenges. The next step would be to create a profile of an ideal partner that would include resources that complement those that the company is able and willing to offer. Returning to the Kericho Project described above, Keys et al. noted that Unilever's strategic challenge was to ensure sustainable supplies of critical raw materials and enhance its corporate reputation and that the strategic challenges for ideal partners were increasing income and skills or rural farmers and ensuring a long-term source of income through sustainable agriculture. The partners were able to achieve their objectives by making the appropriate contributions: Unilever offered ongoing, high-volume purchases of tea (i.e., sustainable incomes), agricultural knowledge, and experience to help improve quality of farming and crops, long-term perspective to allow time to realize mutual benefits, environmental commitment, and reputation and relationships to help build trust with NGOs and governments; and the local partners offered a critical mass of farmers and farming communities motivated to collaborate on activities that would improve sustainability and quality of tea supplies, local and regional government relationships to support improvements in sustainable agriculture, and partners with local energy and habitat-conservation knowledge and experience.

Partnering with Local Nonprofits

One important form of community investment is a partnership between a for-profit business and a local nonprofit organization to collaboratively address a social or environmental issue or cause that neither one of them can adequately address on their own and for which local government has also failed to find a solution. While partnerships between businesses and nonprofit organizations make sense, they can be challenging because they bring together organizations with different ideologies and ways of looking at problems, setting goals, and measuring outcomes. On the other hand, a so-called community business partnership is an excellent opportunity to bring together two or more organizations with common goals and complementary resources to leverage those resources, and the talents and experiences of their employees, to pursue and achieve goals that will benefit the businesses, the nonprofit organizations, and the community.

Each side has different goals and objectives with to any particular community business partnership and companies may provide a range of contributions to the partnership ranging from untied cash grants, workplace giving campaigns, and employee volunteers to more extensive and integrative collaborations involving significant investments of managerial time, reputation, and networking connections. Marketing related sponsorships and cause related marketing initiatives are also popular. In some cases a company and a nonprofit organization may collaborate to conduct research on a particular issue in order to develop new ideas for solutions and disseminate information regarding the issue to governmental agencies and community groups. Businesses and nonprofits may also work together to form and operate social enterprises that are market-based ventures seeking to achieve economic sustainability while fulfilling agreed community-focused social goals. In general, company contributions are intended to provide nonprofit organizations with more stability in their revenue streams, more human resources through the availability of volunteers, and capacity building (i.e., improvements and enhancements to the nonprofit organization's external relations, internal infrastructure, finances, and managerial skills to allow it to more effectively pursue and achieve its core mission).

Research has identified the following common elements of successful community business partnerships:[65]

- Clearly articulated and shared mission with recognized short- and long-term goals and a commitment to a sustainable (i.e., long-term) relationship

---

[65] Adapted from *Enduring Partnerships: Resilience, Innovation, Success* (Boston College Center for Corporate Citizenship, 2005); and Levine, J. 2004. *Elements of Sustainable Partnerships.* Boston College Center for Corporate Citizenship. as cited and discussed in Relationship Matters: Not-for-Profit Community Organizations and Corporate Community Investment (Australian Government Department of Social Services, October 2008), https://dss.gov.au/our-responsibilities/communities-and-vulnerable-people/publications-articles/relationship-matters-not-for-profit-community-organisations-and-corporate-community-investment?HTML#p4

- A commitment of time and funding by the business that reduces the distractions to the nonprofit organization's pursuit of its mission caused by the need to continuously be engaged in fund-raising
- Compatible strategy and values between the partners and mutual recognition of opportunities for both partners arising out of the partnership relationship
- Continual measurement and evaluation of programs, as well as the partnership itself
- Decision making in the best interest of the partnership and to the best interests of each partner
- Good governance and transparency, particularly relating to financial matters
- Identity and integration of the partnership, allowing each partner to separate their individual reputation and brand while integrating the mechanics of the partnership into the structure of each of the participants
- Joint decision making and power sharing, possibly including placing corporate executives on the board of directors of the nonprofit organization
- Ongoing learning, adaptability, and flexibility that allows programs to evolve and the partnership to grow organically
- Open communications by establishing and maintaining mutual trust, as well as anticipating and preventing problems
- Recognition of the various strengths brought to the partnership by each partner (e.g., the sector and program expertise of the nonprofit organization and the measurement and reporting expertise of the for-profit partner)
- Suitable programs that fit with the available resources and core competencies of the partners, organizational size, and location
- Programs that create value and benefits integral to the partnership itself

Companies seeking to enter into business community partnerships must be prepared to engage in thorough and extensive due diligence with respect to prospective partners, realizing that there may be multiple organizations in any given community that appear to be focused on similar goals and objectives. One factor that is particularly important is the willingness and ability of the nonprofit organization to embrace the company's need for accountability and transparency with respect to the operations of the organization due to the obligations that companies have to other stakeholders to account for the ways in which the resources of the company are utilized. Part of the capacity building exercise in forging a business community partnership may be creating a culture of accountability (or improving the existing culture) through the use of key performance indicators tied to explicit deliverable obligations that the nonprofit organization assumes at the time that the partnership is formed.

Building Community Partnerships

While companies often have the functional experience and resources to launch and manage community investments on their own, research has shown that the most effective and impactful investments are carried out with the active engagement and participation of community groups. As such, companies need to be aware of the steps that should be followed in order to implement community partnerships with the ultimate goal of establishing successor organizations managed and controlled by the community as self-sustaining enterprises. While each situation is different, the process generally begins with community engagement that includes the collection of information necessary to determine the appropriate structure for the initial partnership. Once the partnership structure has been established and roles of community groups have been determined, the company can provide training and other resources to build community capacity while the first investment projects are launched. As time goes by, the emphasis should shift to planning and launching successor organizations and setting the appropriate levels of ongoing support to such organizations by the company. Finally, like any business skill or activity, periodic evaluations should be conducted regarding the company's partnership building processes and reports on those processes should be prepared and disseminated throughout the community and to other stakeholders.[66]

Building community partnerships requires information about the local context, information that can be collected using the various community engagement methods typically used such as community meetings, interviews with community leaders, surveys, and the like. The idea at this stage is to map local organizations and understand the priorities and needs within the local community and the resources that are currently available, or lacking, to address the issues that the company is considering for the community partnership initiative. The engagement process provides an opportunity to develop a vision for the partnership and prepare the initial drafts of action plans that will eventually be implemented in the partnership structure. In some cases, the company will actually conduct a small project related to the broader issue area as a way to build confidence within the community and test the potential effectiveness of relationships with community groups that will be critical to the success of the larger partnership. These initial projects are also a good way to get underserved and/or often ignored community groups into the process.

The advantages of early community involvement are well known: fresh perspectives, ability to deliver programs that are more appropriate for community needs and expectations, and creating more support and goodwill within the community. Moreover, if an anticipated investment will require governmental approvals, evidence of community participation in the planning process will usually be necessary before local politicians and administrators can support the project. However, companies should be under no illusion that this stage will be easy, regardless of how much the company believes that it has found an issue upon which the entire community should agree. When the goal is to establish a community partnership, companies need to take into account all of the issues that come up whenever a new organization is launched: conflict resolution and compromise; blending different experiences, cultures and languages into a shared vision and perspective on a particular issue; and designing

---

[66] Portions of the discussion of developing and managing community partnerships herein are adapted from "Developing effective Community Involvement Strategies" published by the Joseph Roundtree Foundation.

a structure for sharing decision making and managing the affairs of the partnership.

One of the first steps in creating community partnerships that will ultimately become self-sustaining is facilitating the launch of a forum that can be used for the various groups within the community with an interest in the issue or project to convene to share information and provide substantial input into the process. A forum of this type is a bit different than the larger public meetings that will likely occur during the engagement process in that they will include representatives from each of the community groups selected for their ability and willingness to engage in a variety of important functions such as electing representatives to the board; nominating representatives to working parties and topic groups; acting as a consultative group for the partnership; managing staff and projects; promoting particular interest groups within the community; and acting as a channel of information.[67]

Having community representatives at the board level ensures that the community has been consulted regarding all important decisions relating to the partnership. Community board representatives should be appointed with the expectation that they will meet regularly with groups throughout the community to inform the community about the status of the partnership's projects and elicit open dialogue with ideas and criticisms that can be brought back to the entire board. Community representatives involved with working parties and topic groups perform similar functions to the community board members within their areas of interest and expertise. For example, working parties can be formed for each of the neighborhoods within the community that will be impacted by the project in order to identify and manage the unique impacts of the project on a particular neighborhood. In some cases, responsibility for implementing and delivering smaller initial projects can be handed over to community representatives in order to build experience and confidence; however, care should be taken to ensure that they have ongoing support from company specialists who can provide advice. When community representatives are part of the governance and management process, special attention needs

---

[67] Id. at 4.

to be paid to ensuring that meetings are conducted in a way that fits the schedule of community members and takes into account their special needs with respect to language, level of formality, access, and day care.

While companies will generally retain a substantial level of input and authority regarding decision making during the earlier stages of a community partnership, this is also the time that investments should be made in training community members and groups so that they can eventually manage projects on their own. In order for partnership to function independent of the company and any one community organization provision should be made for separate office space and equipment. An administrative budget should be created, recognizing that most of the resources will initially come from the company. The partnership should have access to the same types of professional resources as more established community organizations include legal, accounting, and financial service providers. Extensive training should be made available to community members interested in becoming more involved with the management of the partnership and its successor organization and the curriculum should address financial administration, legal duties and obligations and management, leadership, and communications skills.

Once the partnership is up and running and has established a positive track record within the community, it is time to move forward with establishing a successor organization that is self-sustaining and managed principally by the community itself with appropriate, but limited, ongoing support from the original company sponsor. While companies can, and often do, build a large portfolio of community partnerships as part of the community investment strategies, it will ultimately be very difficult for the company to maintain the same level of participation in each of these partnerships. Moreover, companies may wish to shift the focus of the community investments into other areas and will want to withdraw resources from partnerships that have either failed to achieve their purpose or, more positively, are ready to stand on their own as a local community organization. Establishing a successor organization should be part of the partnership planning from the beginning and companies should continuously scan the environment for people and groups who can successfully and seamlessly assume control of partnerships.

There is no single best resource for a successor organization. In some cases the community leaders of the partnership may emerge as the clear best candidates to take over the projects. In other situations the best place to move the activities of the partnership may be an existing community organization that has proven to be a reliable and competent strategic ally of the partnership during various partnership projects. Creating a new community development corporation, as discussed elsewhere in this chapter, is also a viable alternative. Whatever method is selected, the goal should be a strong locally managed organization with both its own assets and a support infrastructure that ensures it will have access to the resources necessary to achieve sustainability. On the second point, the successor organization should have strong relationships with governmental agencies, local nonprofit organizations, and private businesses who would be willing to step in with short-term funding and provide ongoing training.

Community partnering is one of the noblest and more effective methods that companies can deploy in their community investment strategies and it is important for companies to evaluate their partnering activities regularly and include information on community partnering in their sustainability reporting. Reporting should address the purpose and strategy of each of the partnerships and include information on both quantifiable outputs (e.g., number of community members served, community organizations supported) and more intangible outputs such as improvement to community engagement processes. Reporting should also track the progress of the partnership toward the transition to a successor organization. While all partnership programs are important, capacity building should be emphasized in communications with the community. Not to be forgotten is the positive impact of working on partnership initiatives for employees.

Community Development Corporations

Businesses often engage in community economic development activities through sponsorships and other collaborations with local community development corporations (CDCs), which are 501(c)(3) nonprofit organizations that have been formed and organized to support and revitalize communities, especially those that are impoverished or strug-gling.[68] While CDCs have traditionally been active in projects relating to the development of affordable housing by buying, renovating, or build for sale or rental properties, a CDC can be formed to address any specific current need within the community. In many cases, communities may be facing a number of related challenges that appear to fall into differ-ent areas. For example, many cities have large areas within their borders in which the residents feel cut off from the rest of the city due to poor transportation; the housing stock is inadequate and deteriorating due to inattention from absentee landlords; the schools are low performing and inadequately funded; mortality rates are high, particularly from condi-tions that are treatable if health services were readily available; and jobs, amenities, basic recreational opportunities (i.e., clean and safe parks) and core business services (i.e., grocery stores) are lacking. In that situation, the goal and purpose of the CDC is to bring community leaders together to develop solutions, place pressure on policymakers to act, and provide a focal point for contributions of cash and other resources from individuals, businesses, and nonprofit organizations willing and able to assist.

Since communities generally have a number of areas that would ben-efit from the focus of a CDC (e.g., education, job training, health care, commercial development, and other social programs), it is impossible to prepare a list of all the potential activities of a CDC; however, the follow-ing list of CDC activities may be useful in providing ideas:[69]

- Undertaking economic development projects in the commu-nity including developing real estate, attracting businesses, forming new businesses, providing job training, managing sum-mer work programs, revitalizing a commercial district, et cetera.

---

[68] Erekaini, R. 2014. "What Is a Community Development Corporation?" September 17, 2014. https://naceda.org/index.php?option=com_dailyplanet blog&view=entry&category=bright-ideas&id=25%3Awhat-is-a-community-development-corporation-&Itemid=171

[69] Information on additional ideas for CDC activities and programs is available from the National Alliance of Community Economic Development Associations (https://naceda.org/)

- Providing social services (e.g., shelters, community poverty relief, case work, substance abuse programs, social skills, and budgeting training, individual development accounts)
- Assisting neighbors in getting to know each other (i.e., building social capital) or community organizing to get more attention from government and other funders
- Organizing both routine and ambitious clean ups of abandoned buildings, brownfields, or even parks or streams when they are detracting from the health and appearance of the community
- Creating and managing projects to add landscaping, pole banners, public art, mini-parks, and other streetscape features such as new sidewalks or more functional or aesthetic street lighting
- Branding a neighborhood (i.e., new logos, banners, signature events, neighborhood boundaries, and even neighborhood names)

Individuals, groups, and formal organizations, such as existing businesses, may decide to work together to form and operate a CDC to address an identifiable need within a community that has not been met by existing government programs, organizations, for-profit businesses, and/or other nonprofits. In many cases, a CDC is formed after efforts to prod some or all of the entities mentioned in the previous sentence, particularly governmental bodies, to take action and/or reform their operations to address the need have failed. A CDC is not a governmental entity, although many CDCs work closely with representatives of local governments and develop a synergistic relationship with lawmakers and civil servants in the community. CDCs often attract financial support from both public and private sources and while a CDC is a tax-exempt nonprofit there is no specific tax identification or certification that distinguishes a CDC from other nonprofits. CDCs can be quite large, such as well-established organizations in urban communities that have developed and own and operate significant numbers of affordable housing units, or smaller groups that meet in the basement of a school or community center. Staffing for CDCs will usually be a combination of paid workers and volunteers, although the CDC's ability to compensate its staff will obviously depend on the available financial support.

In the typical case, the key steps that are required to plan for and launch a new CDC include the following:[70]

- Defining the community need and geographic boundaries
- Finding like-minded individuals and groups within the community and forming a steering committee to conduct and oversee the preformation process
- Discussing and refining a statement of need and the preferred focus areas for the proposed CDC
- Determining whether the new CDC will duplicate efforts of any existing organization, and if so, trying to collaborate with it (or even simply invest the resources set aside for the new CDC into the existing organization)
- Sharing the vision informally with community members and incorporating their criticisms and priorities in order to identify activities that are likely to garner a high level of interest and support within the community at large
- Providing a face-to-face forum in which interested individuals are invited to learn of the vision of the steering committee
- Thinking about how the new CDC can obtain enough funding to complete one or two early projects and achieve traction in the community
- Finding an attorney and accountant that can support the CDC in the formation and organization process on a pro bono basis
- Recruiting the initial members of the board of directors of the CDC, making sure to have a mix of expertise and

---

[70] Adapted from suggestions made in Useful Community Development, "Why Start a Community Development Corporation?" https://useful-community-development.org/start-a-community-development-corporation.html. The website also includes a large library of resources that can be used to gather information on how to launch community development corporations focusing on specific issue areas such as housing, beautification, and crime prevention.

connections within the local community as well as any other
persons needed to plan and execute the early projects of
the CDC

- Determining the organizational structure of the new CDC
  including decisions regarding types of membership, voting
  rights, advisory boards, et cetera.
- Forming and organizing the new CDC and applying for
  nonprofit status
- Completing an initial project or event to announce the arrival
  of the CDC in the community and provide a basis for reach-
  ing out to community members for support and engagement
- Building the foundation for the bigger, long-term projects
  and initiatives of the CDC through surveys, community
  meetings, and other organizing activities and developing
  fund-raising campaigns
- Developing a long-term strategic plan that describes the major
  proposed projects, resource requirements, sources of funds,
  and community impact goals

While planning for and launching a new CDC, the organizers must
be focused on identifying the unique role that the CDC can play in building a strong, healthier, and more prosperous community by collecting
the expertise, experience, and financial support needed to address the
particular need or problem. A CDC should not be formed for a single
one-time project; instead the organizers must be prepared to make a long-
term commitment and position the CDC as a permanent player in the
economic, social, cultural, and political arenas of the community. The
leaders of the CDC should expect to become strong voices for change and
engage with local institutions, both public and private, and a broad range
of community members.

While a CDC is a nonprofit organization, it must be prepared to create and maintain a sustainable business model in order to develop a steady
stream of funding from both public sources and private investment. This
is particularly important since grant money, while welcome, will seldom
meet all the budgetary needs for a comprehensive economic development
project and local governments as well as the intended beneficiaries of the

project will not be able to provide sufficient financial support.[71] Financial needs will, of course, vary depending on the proposed activities of the CDC (i.e., some projects, such as developing affordable housing, are quite capital intensive while others, such as providing social services, can be effectively carried out with assistance from volunteers). When staffing a CDC, consideration should be given to ensuring diversity and a broad mix of experiences that reflect the backgrounds of those in the community who will be most impacted by the activities of the CDC.[72]

Grants from foundations are one of the most common sources of funding for CDCs and the organizers of the CDC will need to be familiar with the criteria that will be applied by the foundations from which the CDC is likely to request support. Among other things, CDCs must be mindful of the geographic and topical focus of each foundation and the specific process that the foundation uses to receive and review applications (in some cases, foundations operate on an "invitation only" basis, which means that the CDC will need to make connections with people within or affiliated with the foundation first to obtain an invitation from the foundation to submit a proposal). In many situations, businesses collaborate with CDCs through their own charitable foundations; however, in some cases the business may become involved in a project with an expectation of deriving a reasonable return on investment, albeit not as

---

[71] Local government programs are often not highly publicized and CDCs will need to carefully scan for programs in their area that might be related to their topical interest. Areas in which local governments often have some programming include economic opportunity, particularly assistance for small business development; housing (e.g., emergency home repairs, repair loans, down payment assistance, and renters' rights assistance), transportation and neighborhood care and beautification. M. Beeler, C. Kim, and K. Peris, *Starting a Community Development Corporation: A Report Prepared for Colony Park CDC* (University of Texas at Austin, School of Architecture), 17.

[72] Information on forming and operating CDCs corporations is available from a variety of sources such as the Texas Association of Community Development Corporations (https://tacdc.org/), a nonprofit statewide membership association of CDC's and related nonprofit, government, and for-profit entities that provides services, research and advocacy, and events that provide training and allow networking opportunities.

high as might be targeted in an entirely commercial project. For example, providing affordable housing is an area in which CDCs are often involved as part of their efforts to revitalize their communities and this may occur through partnership with for-profit real estate developers. The benefits of these alliances to develop low- and moderate-income housing and/or neighborhood retail centers come from the unique skills and resources each side can bring to the project. As one study of how CDCs can work with for-profit developers pointed out,

> CDCs bring connections to and knowledge of the community, their local economic development mission and expertise, and access to public funding sources, while for-profit developers offer expertise in conventional real estate financing and familiarity with the development process and market demands.[73]

As noted above, a CDC needs a sustainable business model and in order to achieve that the founders and leaders of the CDC must be able to build the requisite organizational capacity to achieve the goals established for the CDC and make the CDC a recognized participant in economic and social development activities in the community. Capacity-building needs and related strategies for a CDC have been summarized as follows:[74]

- *Effective Executive Director*: While the CDC may need to rely on volunteers during the early days and months until more financial support is available, once resources can be found an experienced executive director (ED) should be hired to provide the CDC with a leader who has the skills necessary to build the organization internally and advocate full time on behalf of the CDC in the community and with prospective

---

[73] Myerson, D. October 2002. *Community Development Corporations Working with For-Profit Developers*. Urban Land Institute: Washington DC (includes a summary of recommendation for effective alliances).

[74] Beeler, M., C. Kim, and K. Peris. *Starting a Community Development Corporation: A Report Prepared for Colony Park CDC*, 32. University of Texas at Austin, School of Architecture.

partners. Once the ED has been hired, the board should be attentive to ensuring that he or she is building and maintaining good relations with the board, community leaders, and local politicians.

- *Competent and Stable Staff:* One of the primary responsibilities of the ED is building a competent and stable staff that allows the CDC to grow in a managed fashion with a minimum of turnover among personnel so that community members can build relationships with the people working throughout the community on behalf of the CDC. The CDC needs to offer training and fair compensation (salaries and benefits) commensurate with experience, skills, and commitment to the CDC, although the ED and the board also need to be mindful that higher salaries may be negatively perceived within the community as being inconsistent with the mission of the CDC to serve impoverished members of the community. Non-employee technical specialists should be used as necessary; however, specialists should be used sparingly since they often lack experience in community-related work.

- *Effective Fiscal Management:* Staff hours should be allocated to accounting, budget management, and fiscal planning and staff should be continuously trained in fiscal management skills and tools. Fiscal management is obviously important for any business, but especially for CDCs given their fiduciary duties as nonprofit organizations. Fiscal management, as well as management information systems, allows CDCs to maximize scarce resources through increased efficiency and effectiveness.

- *Board Development and Leadership:* The composition and skills of the board of directors of the CDC is crucial to success and every effort should be made, from the very beginning, to bring together a board that is diverse in all aspects: gender, ethnicity, talents, experiences, and connections. Diversity in all of these areas stretches the reach of the CDC well beyond the cash and tangible assets at hand and should enable to board to create a shared vision for the CDC that can be supported by clearly articulated objectives.

- *Managed Growth*: A CDC may be formed and launched around a single project; however, for sustainability to occur, it is necessary to review the performance of the organization on a regular basis to assess operational needs and, if appropriate, make changes to strategy and projects.
- *Project Management*: Consistent with effective fiscal management is the need to develop and practice sound project management techniques to monitor time and efficiencies of work on projects supported by the CDC and think strategically across all of the CDCs activities. Project management tools should be used to control costs and ensure the quality and affordability of projects.
- *Evaluation*: Each project in which the CDC is involved must include a formal evaluation process designed with input from the CDC to ensure that all appropriate data is gathered and analyzed.

CHAPTER 5

Reporting

As with all aspects of sustainability reporting, practices of companies regarding their disclosures relating to community engagement and investment have been evolving as time has passed and stakeholder interest in such activities has increased. Although mandatory reporting requirements have been slow to emerge, the need to keep communities informed has found its way into global standards such as the OECD Guidelines for Multinational Enterprises (http://mneguidelines.oecd.org/), which provide that enterprises are expected to ensure that timely, regular, reliable, and relevant information is disclosed to the community regarding the activities, structure, financial situation, and performance of the enterprise and relationships between the enterprise and its stakeholders; and communicate information to the community regarding the social, ethical, and environmental policies of the enterprise and other codes of conduct to which the enterprise subscribes (including voluntary standards relating to community involvement and development).

A useful reference point was provided by the Global Reporting Initiative (GRI) (www.globalreporting.org), which is the well-known multistakeholder developed international independent organization that helps businesses, governments, and other organizations understand and communicate the impact of business on critical sustainability issues such as climate change, human rights, corruption, and many others. GRI pioneered sustainability reporting since the late 1990s, transforming it from a niche practice to one now adopted by a growing majority of organizations. GRI's Sustainability Reporting Standards are the most widely used standards on sustainability reporting and disclosure around the world and available for use by public agencies, firms, and other organizations wishing to understand and communicate aspects of their economic, social, and environmental performance.

Reporting on Community Activities in the GRI Framework

The GRI reporting framework has become the most widely accepted template for sustainability reporting. The framework covers a wide range of performance indicators and disclosure standards in three categories: economic, environmental, and social. Organizations that have adopted the GRI framework are expected, among other things, to make disclosures regarding the impact that their investments and other support of infrastructure and local services has had on their stakeholders and the economy; the indirect economic impacts their operations and activities have had on their communities; community investment activities; engagement with local communities; the actual and potential negative impacts of their actions on local communities and their managerial approach to community issues.

GRI Disclosure Standard 201: Economic Performance

GRI 201 is concerned with the topic of economic performance of reporting organizations and includes, among other things, requirements and guidelines with respect to reporting on "direct economic value generated and distributed" by the organization.[1] The reporting requirements in Disclosure 201-1 on economic value distributed explicitly call for disclosures relating to "community investments." The Guidance to Disclosure 201-1 provides that reported investments must be actual expenditures during the reporting period and not just commitments, and that community investments include both voluntary donations and other investments of funds in the broader community where the intended beneficiaries are external to the organization.[2]

Examples of items that normally should be included when reporting include contributions to charities, NGOs, and research institutions (provided that such contributions are unrelated to the organization's own

---

[1] GRI 201: Economic Performance 2016 (Amsterdam: Global Sustainability Standards Board, 2016), 6.

[2] Id. at 7.

commercial research and development); funds to support community infrastructure, such as recreational facilities; and direct costs of social programs, including arts and educational events. With respect to funding for infrastructure projects, organizations are allowed to include capital costs, costs of goods and labor, and operating costs incurred in connection with providing ongoing support for facilities or programs. This means that organizations should include the amount of funding provided for the daily operations of public facilities.[3]

The purpose of any particular investment is obviously important in determining whether or not it should be reported and organizations cannot include expenditures that are legal and commercial activities or where the purpose of the expenditure is exclusively commercial. In the same vein, community investments do not include any infrastructure investment driven primarily by core business needs of the organization or to facilitate the organization's business operations (e.g., building a road to a mine or other business facility). However, organizations can include and report infrastructure investments outside of the main business activities of the organization such as the costs associated with erecting and maintaining schools or hospitals used by the organization's workers and their families.[4] Where significant, organizations should report community investments separately at country, regional, or market levels, and describe the criteria used in order to define and determine significance.

The types of activities that fall within the definition of "community investment" for purposes of meeting the disclosure requirements of GRI 201 were covered in a variety of ways in the 72 sustainability reports reviewed and analyzed in 2008 by the GRI working in collaboration with the University of Hong Kong and CSR Asia (the GRI Reporting Survey).[5] For example, along with education and training, philanthropy and charitable giving was one of the two most covered topics in the analyzed reports, appearing in 63 percent of the reports.

---

[3] Id.

[4] Id.

[5] Reporting on Community Impacts: A survey conducted by the Global Reporting Initiative, the University of Hong Kong and CSR Asia (Amsterdam: Stichting Global Reporting Initiative, 2008), 4.

The topic was described as reporting focusing on in-kind and cash donations to charitable organizations.[6] Companies reported on a fairly robust
set of performance indicators with respect to philanthropy and charitable
giving including the following (the top three being the indicators most
commonly found):

- Sum of money donated, raised, contributed to community
  initiatives
- Percentage or number of people/organizations benefited by
  the services supported by donation from the company
- Number or quantity of scholarships/material/services donated
  (value of the donated scholarships, material, services not indicated)
- Value (i.e., in terms of money) of material donated
- Percentage of pre-tax profits donated

Reporting on philanthropy and charitable giving also included several
impact indicators such as:

- Number of homes rebuilt/number of families formed
- The income by the community member received from the
  sales of products
- Percentage drop in infant mortality
- Percentage rise in community members receiving access to
  education
- Number of children that are free from malnutrition
- Percentage of villages rebuilt

Philanthropy and charitable giving has been the traditional method
for supporting social and environmental causes in local communities. In
additional to financial support, more and more businesses are expanding
their contributions to include managerial support in order to enhance the
capacity of locally driven nonprofit organizations with sustainable devel-
opment-focused missions.[7]

---

[6] Id. at 29 and 33.

[7] How 17 Companies Are Tackling Sustainable Development Goals (and Your
Company Can, Too) http://sdgfunders.org/blog/how-17-companies-are-tack-
ling-sustainable-development-goals-and-your-company-can-too/

Total community investment expenditure was also among the five most frequently covered topics in the reports analyzed for the GRI Reporting Survey, appearing in 46 percent of the reports. The topic was described as including reporting that focuses on the overall expenditure of the company's spending on various community initiatives.[8] Companies reported on a fairly robust set of performance indicators with respect to total community investment expenditure including the following (the top three being the indicators most commonly found):

- Sum of money spent on community investment
- Percentage of profit/revenue/income spent on community investment
- Percentage increase of money spent on social investment, when compared to last year
- Number of people benefited in community investment activities
- Number of social investment projects developed and completed

Notably, however, the reporting companies generally failed to identify and report on any impacts from their community investment expenditures.

Also relevant to community investment (as well as engagement, discussed further below), although not specifically mentioned in GRI 201, is community services and volunteering, which was covered in 49 percent of the reports analyzed for the GRI Survey, thus making it one of the five most frequently covered topics in those reports. The topic was described as including reporting that focuses on the involvement of both the company and its employees in community actions.[9] Companies reported on a fairly robust set of performance indicators with respect to community

---

[8] Reporting on Community Impacts: A survey conducted by the Global Reporting Initiative, the University of Hong Kong and CSR Asia (Amsterdam: Stichting Global Reporting Initiative, 2008), 30 and 33.

[9] Id. at 29 and 33.

services and employee volunteering including the following (the top three being the indicators most commonly found):

- Number of people/organizations benefited or served, or number of volunteering projects implemented
- Number of volunteers from the company
- Number of volunteering hours offered by employees
- Number of employees sent for community service, amount of equipment/resources provided for community service
- Number/amount of items distributed or built by the community service
- Amount of funds raised or donated
- Community service participation rate by employees/company operations
- Number of service councils/committees formed
- Proportion of volunteering day entitlements taken up by employees

Notably, however, the reporting companies generally failed to identify and report on any impacts from their community services and employee volunteering. The researchers who prepared the report speculated that the failure of the companies to measure the impact of volunteering activities on the community might be traced to a feeling among companies that the most significant benefits to companies from their volunteering programs come from strengthening ties between employee perception of a company's impact on the community and employee morale and retention.[10]

A related topic, reported on by 18 percent of the reporting companies covered by the GRI Reporting Survey, was partnerships with local organizations, which included reporting that focused on partnerships with and/or participation in certain organizations in the community. Performance indicators for this topic included the sum of money donated to partners or spent on partnerships; the number of partnering organizations; the number of people benefited; the number of projects worked in partnership; and the value of goods donated. Unfortunately, as was the case with

---

[10] Id. at 10.

reporting on community services and employee volunteering, companies failed to identify and report on any impacts from their community partnering initiatives.[11]

Finally, 10 percent of the reports analyzed for the GRI Reporting Survey included coverage of sponsorships and cause-related marketing campaigns, which were described as including in-kind or cash sponsorship on community initiatives resulting in the display of company name and logo in the initiatives.[12] The performance indicators that companies reported on with respect to cause-related marketing included the number of people/organizations benefited; the sum of money donated for sponsorships; and the number of events supported. No impact indicators were identified and reported on with respect to cause-related marketing activities.

GRI Disclosure Standard 203: Indirect Economic Impacts

The economic dimension of sustainability in the context of the GRI standards is not concerned about the financial condition of organizations but instead focuses on the impact that an organization makes on its stakeholders and on economic systems at the local, national, and global level. The GRI reporting system incorporates disclosures on direct economic impacts, which are defined as a change in the productive potential of the economy that has an influence on a community's or stakeholder's well-being and longer-term prospects for development, and indirect economic impacts, which are the additional consequences of the direct impact of financial transactions and the flow of money between an organization and its stakeholders and can be monetary or nonmonetary.[13]

---

[11] Id. at 29 and 33.

[12] Id. at 29 and 33.

[13] The GRI anticipates that the information that an organization uses to prepare its economic disclosures will be compiled using figures from its audited financial statements or from its internally audited management accounts and that data will be compiled based on the application of internationally recognized financial reporting standards. GRI 203: Indirect Economic Impacts 2016 (Amsterdam: Global Sustainability Standards Board, 2016), 6.

GRI 203 calls on organizations to describe their managerial approach to the indirect economic impacts of their operations including a discussion of the work undertaken by the organization to understand indirect economic impacts at the national, regional, or local level and an explanation of whether the organization conducted a community needs assessment to determine the need for infrastructure and other services (and, assuming such an assessment was done, a description of the results of the assessment).[14] Specific disclosures required under GRI 203 must address indirect economic impacts as well as the impact of an organization's infrastructure investments and services supported. The commentary to GRI 203 emphasizes that the assessment process described above is particularly important in relation to local communities and regional economies and the quality of disclosures relating to the process is discussed in more detail below.[15]

GRI Disclosure 203-1 is concerned with the impact that an organization's infrastructure investments and services supported have on its stakeholders and the economy and calls for reporting organizations to report the extent of development of significant infrastructure investments and services supported; current or expected impacts on communities and local economies, including positive and negative impacts where relevant; and whether these investments and services are commercial, in-kind, or pro bono engagements.[16] GRI 203 recommended that when reporting organizations are compiling the information specified in Disclosure 203-1 they should disclose the size, cost, and duration of each significant infrastructure investment or service supported; and the extent to which different communities or local economies are impacted by the organization's infrastructure investments and services supported (e.g., the number of persons in the community who benefited from the organization's support of community services). The impact of infrastructure investments can extend beyond the scope of the organization's own operations and is typically felt over a long timescale. Examples of potentially impactful infrastructure investments provided in GRI 203 included transport

---

[14] Id. at 5.

[15] Id. at 4.

[16] Id. at 6.

links, utilities, community social facilities, health and welfare centers, and sports centers.

Thirty-two percent of the reports analyzed for the GRI Reporting Survey included coverage of infrastructure for local community, making that topic the tenth most popular out of 17 topics. The topic was described as including reporting on construction or provision of infrastructure for the benefit of the community (e.g., housing, roads, recreational facilities, etc.).[17] The performance indicators that companies reported on with respect to infrastructure for the local community included the number of people/families/organization/communities benefited; the number/area/length of facilities built; the sum of money invested or value of construction material donated; the number of infrastructure projects involved; the percentage of sewage effluent recycled; and the volume of potable water produced. No impact indicators were identified and reported on with respect to local community infrastructure initiatives.

GRI Disclosure 203-2 is concerned with the spectrum of indirect economic impacts that an organization can have on its stakeholders and the economy and requires that reporting organizations report examples of significant identified indirect economic impacts of the organization, including positive and negative impacts, and describe the significance of the indirect economic impacts in the context of external benchmarks and stakeholder priorities, such as national and international standards, protocols, and policy agendas.[18] Examples of significant indirect economic impacts, both positive and negative, provided in in GRI 203 included:[19]

- Changes in the productivity of organizations, sectors, or the whole economy (such as through greater adoption of information technology)

---

[17] Reporting on Community Impacts: A survey conducted by the Global Reporting Initiative, the University of Hong Kong and CSR Asia (Amsterdam: Stichting Global Reporting Initiative, 2008), 29 and 33.

[18] GRI 203: Indirect Economic Impacts 2016 (Amsterdam: Global Sustainability Standards Board, 2016), 7.

[19] Id.

- Economic development in areas of high poverty (such as changes in the total number of dependents supported through the income of a single job)
- Economic impacts of improving or deteriorating social or environmental conditions (such as changing job market in an area converted from small farms to large plantations, or the economic impacts of pollution)
- Availability of products and services for those on low incomes (such as preferential pricing of pharmaceuticals, which contributes to a healthier population that can participate more fully in the economy; or pricing structures that exceed the economic capacity of those on low incomes)
- Enhanced skills and knowledge in a professional community or in a geographic location (such as when shifts in an organization's needs attract additional skilled workers to an area, who, in turn, drive a local need for new learning institutions)
- Number of jobs supported in the supply or distribution chain (such as the employment impacts on suppliers as a result of an organization's growth or contraction)
- Stimulating, enabling, or limiting foreign direct investment (such as when an organization changes the infrastructure or services it provides in a developing country, which then leads to changes in foreign direct investment in the region)
- Economic impacts from a change in operation or activity location (such as the impact of outsourcing jobs to an overseas location)
- Economic impacts from the use of products and services (such as economic growth resulting from the use of a particular product or service)

GRI Disclosure Standard 413: Local Community Engagement and Impacts

GRI 413 addresses disclosures relating to a reporting organization's engagement with local communities and actual and potential negative

impacts of the organization's actions on local communities.[20] GRI 413
calls for reporting organizations to discuss their management approach
to local communities by describing the means by which stakeholders are
identified and engaged with; which vulnerable groups have been identified; any collective or individual rights that have been identified that are
of particular concern for the community in question; how it engages with
stakeholder groups that are particular to the community (for example,
groups defined by age, indigenous background, ethnicity or migration
status); and the means by which its departments and other bodies address
risks and impacts, or support independent third parties to engage with
stakeholders and address risks and impacts.[21]

The GRI reporting requirements with respect to local communities
reflect a keen interest in identifying and managing actual and potential
negative impacts, as discussed in more detail below, and in order for
impact management to be effective an organization must have processes
for assessment and planning in order to under the actual and potential
impacts and practice strong engagement with the local communities in
which it operates in order to understand their needs and expectations.[22]
The reporting requirements for Disclosure 413-1 are intended to elicit
information on assessment, planning, and engagement by asking organizations to disclose the percentage of operations with implemented and
consistently applied local community engagement, impact assessments,
and/or development programs including the use of the following key
elements of an effective program:[23]

- Social impact assessments, including gender impact assessments, based on participatory processes
- Environmental impact assessments and ongoing monitoring
- Public disclosure of results of environmental and social impact
  assessments

---

[20] GRI 413: Local Communities 2016 (Amsterdam: Global Sustainability
Standards Board, 2016).
[21] Id. at 6.
[22] Id. at 7.
[23] Id. at 7–8.

- Local community development programs based on local communities' needs
- Stakeholder engagement plans based on stakeholder mapping
- Broad based local community consultation committees and processes that include vulnerable groups
- Works councils, occupational health and safety committees, and other worker representation bodies to deal with impacts
- Formal local community grievance processes

The preliminary guidance in GRI 413 begins by requiring reporting organizations to describe their management approach to identification and engagement of stakeholders among the local communities in which the organization operates and the specific guidance for Disclosure 413-1 goes on to make it clear that the GRI believes that establishing a timely and effective stakeholder identification and engagement process is important to help organizations understand the vulnerability of local communities and how these might be affected by the organization's activities.[24] The preferred approach is to implement the stakeholder engagement process early in the planning stages and to maintain the process as operations in the local community evolve. Early engagement provides organizations with the best opportunity to elicit the views of community stakeholders in decision making, address potential adverse impacts on local communities in advance and before they rise to crisis levels, and establish lines of communication between an organization's various departments (i.e., planning, finance, environment, production, etc.) and key stakeholder interest groups in the local community.[25]

The guidance for Disclosure 413-1 also emphasizes the use and importance of social and human rights impact assessment tools during the engagement process as an effective means for ensuring that stakeholders are identified and that organizations have a solid understanding of the relevant characteristics of the members of their local community such as ethnic background, indigenous descent, gender, age, migrant status, socioeconomic status, literacy levels, disabilities,

---

[24] Id. at 7.
[25] Id. at 8.

income level, infrastructure availability, or specific human health vulnerabilities.[26]

Identification of and engagement with vulnerable or disadvantaged groups is raised as a particular concern in the guidance for Disclosure 413-1 and reporting organizations are expected to make disclosures regarding steps that may have been taken to adopt differentiated measures to allow the effective participation of vulnerable groups, such as making information available in alternate languages or format for those who are not literate or who do not have access to printed materials. The guidance also makes it clear that, when necessary, reporting organizations are expected to establish additional or separate processes so that negative impacts on vulnerable or disadvantaged groups are avoided, minimized, mitigated, or compensated.[27]

Finally, while the ideal situation would be for organizations to anticipate and avoid negative impacts from operations on local communities, the reality is that this may be not be possible or that residual impacts will remain after efforts to mitigate. In those situations, organizations are expected to continue managing the impacts appropriately, establish effective and timely grievance procedures, and provide local communities with fair compensation for negative impacts.[28]

Community engagement and dialogue was among the five most frequently covered topics in the reports analyzed for the GRI Reporting Survey, appearing in 46 percent of the reports. The topic was described as including reporting that focuses on the process of communicating with stakeholders in the community.[29] Companies reported on a fairly robust set of performance indicators with respect to community engagement and dialogue including the following (the top three being the indicators most commonly found):

- Number of visitors, audience, or participants reached in the engagement

---

[26] Id.

[27] Id.

[28] Id. at 7.

[29] Reporting on Community Impacts: A survey conducted by the Global Reporting Initiative, the University of Hong Kong and CSR Asia (Amsterdam: Stichting Global Reporting Initiative, 2008), 30 and 33.

- Percentage/number of operation sites that have community engagement activities
- Frequency of engagement meeting
- Number of people interviewed/surveyed
- Number of engagement workshops or exhibitions conducted
- Amount of project profit shared with community partner
- Number of people who received financial assistance

Reporting on community engagement and dialogue also included the number of complaints received as the sole impact indicator.

GRI Disclosure 413-2 calls on organizations to report on several aspects of significant actual and potential negative impacts on local communities related to an organization's operations, as opposed to the organization's community investments or donations, which should be addressed in disclosures responsible to GRI 201: Economic Performance.[30] First, reporting organizations should report the vulnerability and risk to local communities from potential negative impacts due to factors including the degree of physical or economic isolation of the local community; the level of socioeconomic development, including the degree of gender equality within the community; the state of socioeconomic infrastructure, including health and education infrastructure; the proximity to operations; the level of social organization; and the strength and quality of the governance of local and national institutions around local communities.[31]

Second, reporting organizations should report the exposure of the local community to its operations due to higher than average use of shared resources or impact on shared resources, including the use of hazardous substances that impact the environment and human health in general, and specifically impact reproductive health; the volume and type of pollution released; the status as major employer in the local community; land conversion and resettlement; and natural resource consumption.[32] Many

---

[30] GRI 413: Local Communities 2016 (Amsterdam: Global Sustainability Standards Board, 2016), 9.

[31] Id.

[32] Id.

communities have thrived due to the benevolent presence of a single large business that provides employment opportunities for community members and contributes to local well-being through tax payments and support of infrastructure projects; however, there is obviously potential for abuse that can have harmful impacts in the community. For example, local governmental officials may be reluctant to adopt and/or enforce environmental regulations to limit adverse impacts on the local habitat from a company's operations due to concerns that the company might decide to move all or a larger portion of its activities elsewhere. Reliance on one large employer may also inhibit development of new skills within the community that may be valuable over the long term yet not immediately aligned with the needs of the employer and the markets and sectors in which it operates (e.g., local workers may continue to focus on maturing technology and ignore the need for learning in new technologies that might support development of the community in ways that are different from the incumbent large employer).

Finally, for each of the significant actual and potential negative economic, social, cultural, and/or environmental impacts on local communities and their rights that have been identified and described, reporting organizations should go on to describe the intensity or severity of the impact; the likely duration of the impact; the reversibility of the impact; and the scale of the impact.[33] Compliance with this requirement raises challenging issues for companies that might be concerned about the legal risks associated with conveying information to the public regarding their behavior processes and other aspects of its operations related to its environmental compliance and social performance. For example, investors and consumer advocates often seize on the disclosures that companies make regarding their struggles in addressing environmental and social issues to bring lawsuits against those companies or otherwise exert public pressure on the companies to make changes at a pace and cost that are beyond the company's immediate resources. While the legal risks of such disclosures can never be totally eliminated, companies can and should manage their mandatory and voluntary sustainability

---

[33] Id.

reporting by making sure that their disclosures and other related communications are consistent, accurate, and include a balanced presentation of risks and the reasonable steps that the company intends to remediate those risks.[34]

The guidance for GRI Disclosure 413-2 emphasizes that the disclosures are intended to inform stakeholders about an organization's awareness of its negative impacts on local communities and it is expected that the information required to make the disclosures can be readily accessed from data already compiled and analyzed in order to make disclosures for a number of other GRI topics such as Indirect Economic Impacts (GRI 203); Materials (GRI 301); Energy (GRI 302); Water (GRI 303); Biodiversity (GRI 304); Emissions (GRI 305); Effluents and Waste (GRI 306); Occupational Health and Safety (GRI 403); Child Labor (GRI 408): Forced or Compulsory Labor (GRI 409); Security Practices (GRI 410); Rights of Indigenous Peoples (GRI 411); and Customer Health and Safety (GRI 416). Internal risk assessments can and should also be used to create appropriate priorities for allocation of time, resources, and investment to address and mitigate negative impacts.[35]

Reporting on Management Approach to Community Development

The GRI standards have long called on companies to provide a description of their management approach to community issues. In fact, as noted above, GRI 203 calls on organizations to describe their managerial approach to the indirect economic impacts of their operations including a discussion of the steps taken to assess community needs with respect to infrastructure and other services. Unfortunately, most companies have failed to comply, perhaps because they have not taken the time to develop organization wide principles and policies regarding community involvement and/or establish specific goals. In fact, the GRI Reporting Survey found that only a few

---

[34] For further discussion, see S. Orr, *The Legal Risks Associated with Corporate Sustainability Reporting* (Latham & Watkins LLP, July 23, 2015), https://lw.com/ thoughtLeadership/corporate-sustainability-reporting-associated-legal-risks
[35] GRI 413: Local Communities 2016 (Amsterdam: Global Sustainability Standards Board, 2016), 10.

companies were able to clearly define corporate goals regarding community performance, in most cases providing statements of goals that were usually very vague and could not be easily measured. The GRI Reporting Survey also noted that less than half of the reporting companies reported on the availability of an organizational policy that defined the company's over-all commitment to the community.[36] Companies were even more remiss with respect to reporting on other aspects of management of community involvement with less than one in five providing information on what should be basic and essential matters such as identifying the senior position with operational responsibility for community-related issues, training, and raising of awareness with respect to community issues and monitoring and follow-up with respect to community issues.[37]

Drawing on the best examples from the reports surveyed to prepare the GRI Reporting Survey, the GRI and its collaborators inferred that compa-nies should provide substantial information on their managerial approaches and policies toward every community issue material to the operations in a separate section and should also indicate how those approaches and policies are incorporated into their management standards. This discussion should separately identify the relevant issues (e.g., community development, social economic impacts, protecting the culture and rights of indigenous peoples, community investment, charitable giving, and employee volunteering). Actual reporting in relation to each of these issues should be laid out in another section of the report with the narration in each section being sup-ported by case studies, testimonials, and other illustrative tools.[38]

Most companies that were assessed during the GRI Reporting Sur-vey failed to provide a clear and meaningful description of their goals with respect to performance in relation to the communities in which they operate. In many cases, the companies simply used vague and general platitudes such as "being a good neighbor," "working with local people," and making the communities "a better place to live." Those companies

---

[36] Reporting on Community Impacts: A survey conducted by the Global Report-ing Initiative, the University of Hong Kong and CSR Asia (Amsterdam: Stichting Global Reporting Initiative, 2008), 22.

[37] Id. at 23.

[38] Id. at 22.

that did a good job with respect to reporting on goals laid their objectives out clearly, established targets that could easily be understood and measured, and, in those cases where the targets were long term, described the specific progress that the company had made during the reporting period. An example for one company included in the GRI Reporting Survey established a goal to develop and maintain a consistent approach to data capture and annual monitoring of community social investment spending and project evaluation. The target in that case is to put in place a start-of-the-art electronic reporting application, a process that would likely take a few years; however, after stating the target the company could then provide an update for the current period that made sense in terms of progression toward the goal (i.e., completion of a comprehensive survey of community social investment at all sites).[39]

Companies have been slow to create and publish organization wide policies with respect to their community activities and overall commitment to involvement and investment in their communities. Those companies that do have policies have taken two approaches. In some cases, the policy is used a means for communicating principles in relation to community commitment (i.e., commitments to be respectful of the rights and interests of community members, communicate, and consult with the community and work with the community to ensure that the company's operations provide meaningful benefits to community stakeholders). The second strategy with respect to policymaking is to focus on how the company intends to contribute to the community and identify a particular issue that the company will address along with the types of support that will be provided (e.g., improving the future prospects of children by supporting education, culture, and sporting activities and conservation of natural resources).[40]

LBG Framework for Measuring Corporate Community Investment

LBG (www.lbg-online.net/), which is managed by Corporate Citizenship, a global corporate responsibility consultancy based in London with offices in

---

[39] Id.
[40] Id. at 22–23.

Singapore and New York, is intended to be the global standard for measuring "corporate community investment." LBG's vision is a world where every business measures its community investment and shares this is an open, transparent, and consistent way, and its mission is to provide a platform of LBG members to work with each other, and with their partners in the community, to improve measurement, share best practices and new ideas, and make a greater difference.[41] Businesses may apply the LBG measurement framework in order to take advantage of a consistent approach to measuring, benchmarking, and reporting on their corporate community investment activities. The framework is designed to help businesses quantify its "inputs," which include what they contribute to communities, the resulting "outputs" (i.e., what happened within the community and with respect to the business) and understand and explain the impact of its activities (i.e., the changes that the contributions made for the community and for the business itself). According to LBG, over 200 companies from all over the world have voluntarily engaged in the LBG network to apply, develop, and enhance the framework.[42] Businesses can use LBG framework to inform management decisions about the future direction of their community activity, understand how their own community activity compares with peers and/or "best-in-class" companies and communicate results to key audiences.[43]

LBG noted that while businesses engage in a wide range of activities that have a positive impact on society and contribute to sustainability including creation of wealth and jobs, delivery of goods and services, payment of taxes, and support for innovation, corporate community investment can and should be distinguished. According to LBG, corporate community investment should be defined and understood as including "voluntary engagement with charitable organizations and activities that extends beyond companies' core business activities."[44] This definition

---

[41] *From Inputs to Impact: Measuring Corporate Community Contributions through the LBG Framework—A Guidance Manual* (London: Corporate Citizenship, 2014), 3. The initiative was initially referred to as the "London Benchmarking Group."

[42] Id. at 6.

[43] Id. at 8.

[44] Id. at 4.

includes two key questions for determining if a particular contribution or activity falls into the category of corporate community investment: "Is it voluntary?" *and* "Is it charitable?".[45] As to the question of "voluntariness," the threshold is that the contribution or activity must be something that a business chooses to do and is not mandated under any legal or contractual obligation. In addition, the activity should be outside of the core business activities of the company, which means that using less energy or protecting the health and safety of employees, each hallmarks of a socially responsible business, would not be considered a corporate community investment. In order for the second condition to be satisfied the support must be given to "an organization or activity that is recognized in its geographical location and cultural context as having a clear charitable purpose (e.g., advancing education, protecting health or supporting human rights)."[46]

Examples of contributions and activities that would qualify as a corporate community contribution include a cash donation to a local registered charity; support of education through a program that allows employees to use some of their paid time to participate in a reading partnership with an inner-city school; and running a program in partnership with a charity to provide work experience and training to homeless people. Supporting the socially responsible actions of others, such as when an airline encourages passengers to donate their unused foreign currency to an international NGO when returning home from a trip abroad, also qualifies; however, the airline's reporting on this activity should separate the contributions by passengers from its own contribution so that the airline does not take undue credit beyond the value that its leverage provided to the NGO.

LBG advised companies that application of its framework called for going beyond the assessment of individual activities to enabling businesses to pursue and achieve an appropriate balance of its contributions

---

[45] Id. at 3.

[46] LBG pointed out that there is no single internationally agreed definition of charitable purpose and that reference needs to be made to applicable laws and guidelines relating to charities and tax-exempt charitable organizations in specific jurisdictions. For that reason, LBG focuses on the purpose of the contribution/activity (i.e., its intent and outcome) and not simply the legal status of the beneficiary. Id. at 4–5.

across its entire program in order to realize benefits for individuals within the community and inside the company, community organizations, and the company itself. The framework is intended to prod companies to catalog and measure their contributions and identify and assess what happens as a result of those contributions in order to understand what has been done in the past and improve on future efforts. LBG urged companies to integrate measurement into their planning and management processes for community involvement and investment; develop an effective measurement approach; focus on measuring what matters most (i.e., a small set of key indicators that matter most to the company's program and the company's stakeholders); and resist trying to measure too much and focus instead on the projects and activities that are most aligned with the company's community strategy and data that can be collected easily and readily applied to the company's strategic processes.[47]

LBG cautioned businesses using the framework that it was an art and not a science and should not be approached in the same way as laboriously entering the figures required for a tax return. While using actual costs or achievements obviously leads to clearer reporting, there are times when it is necessary and acceptable to rely on estimates based on accepted methodologies when determining broader valuations (e.g., the cost of employee time spent on volunteering and other community activities). LBG also recommended that it is "better to under-report than over-report" and that businesses should take a conservative approach and leave out activities that are not clearly corporate community investment contributions. Businesses should remember that anything that do include in their reporting will be subject to challenge and criticism by opponents of the any aspect of the operations of the company. Businesses should also guard against trying to measure everything lest the framework become more of an impediment to contributions than a useful tool to help assess and improve what really matters to the company and its communities. Finally, in the same vein, LBG recommends that when businesses first apply the framework they should focus on larger projects or operations—things that are likely to involve substantial inputs and outputs—and

---

[47] Id. at 27–28.

other activities for which information can be easily captured. According to LBG, a good rule of thumb is that the first 80 percent of a company's community contribution takes about 20 percent of the time to compile, a realization that hopefully makes it easier for companies to consider making the investment of time and effort required to implement that framework. A related suggestion for companies is to concentrate first on inputs, which are easier to identify and measure, before getting too involved in the relatively more challenging task of measuring the impacts of the company's corporate community investments.[48]

LBG explained its framework as being "a simple input output model, enabling any [corporate community investment] activity to be assessed consistently in terms of the resources committed and the results achieved."[49] Applying the framework begins with inputs (i.e., what resources did the company provide to support a community activity), continues with outputs (i.e., what happened within the community and the company as a result of the activity and what additional resources were brought to bear on a particular issue as a result of the company's contributions and participation in the activity), and finishes with identifying and measuring the impacts achieved (i.e., the changes that occurred for people, organizations, and the environment within the community and for the involved employees and overall business of the company).

Inputs

Application of the LBG framework begins with measuring "inputs," which are the resources that a company provides to support a community activity or activities. In order to facilitate effective planning and robust reporting, the framework calls for companies to address several different questions:[50]

- *How* is the contribution being made (i.e., cash, paid working time, in-kind contributions, management costs, or a combination thereof)

---

[48] Id. at 7–8.

[49] Id. at 6.

[50] Id. at 10.

- *Why* is the contribution being made (possibilities include philanthropic donations, strategic partnership, and/or commercially driven engagement)
- *What* issue is being addressed/supported by the contribution (e.g., education, health, social welfare, economic development etc.)
- *Where* is the activity taking place (i.e., the geographic scope of the supported activity)

How

As to the first question regarding inputs—how does the company contribute—four different types of contributions should be identified and tracked: cash contributions; time contributions; in-kind contributions of product, property, or services; and management costs, which could include corporate community investment program staff salaries, benefits/overhead, research, and communications.[51] The total cost to the company of engaging in a particular community activity will include one or more of these four types of contributions, each of which raises specific calculation and valuation issues that should be addressed using certain guidelines developed and disseminated by LBG.

In general, identification of cash contributions should be relatively straightforward and LBG mentioned that this category can include direct donations/grants to charitable organizations or activities; social sponsorship of cultural events or institutions (e.g., museums); matching employee giving; covering the expenses of employee involvement; paying for a new facility or service (e.g., a website) for a community organization; membership and subscriptions to community organizations; and the amount that a charity receives from cause-related marketing initiatives if it comes off the company's own bottom line (i.e., if a customer pays a premium which goes to charity, this should not be included as a company contribution, but should be included as "leverage" when reporting outputs). LBG advised that companies should not count contributions to community activities that come from other sources (e.g., employees, customers,

---

[51] Id.

and other organizations), although these may be reportable as leverage in outputs; commercial, as opposed to social, sports sponsorships (i.e., teams with national or international name recognition) or the advertising expenses of a cause-related marketing campaign (the amount actually received by the charity should, of course, be counted).[52]

LBG described a time contribution as being the cost to the company of the *paid* working hours that are contributed by employees to a community organization or activity. Employee "volunteering" is the most obvious example of this type of contribution; however, the category should be more broadly construed to include any active engagement in community activity during paid working time such as active participation in fund-raising activities, longer-term secondments to community organizations, and supervision of work experience placements.[53] LBG provided extensive guidance on methodology for calculating the cost of employee time, including reference to information compiled internally by the company's human resources and finance departments and/or labor data from national statistics organizations; however, the guiding principle should be establishing a figure that most accurately reflects the true cost to the company of an employee actively participating in a community activity during paid working time.

In-kind contributions are another way that companies can contribute noncash resources to community activities. Examples of in-kind contributions that should be counted under the LBG framework include donations of the company's products; provision of pro bono legal, accounting,

---

[52] Id. at 11. For more on potentially difficult issues for identifying, calculating, and reporting on cash contributions, see LBG guidance notes on advertising purchases in charity/community magazines or programs; business services bought from community organizations; carbon offset payments; cause-related marketing; company matching of employee giving and fundraising; corporate foundations; donations via government; employee involvement (volunteering) expenses; energy efficiency commitments; memberships and subscriptions to community organizations; payments to vulnerable customers; sponsorship of arts/cultural events; commercial sponsorship of events, publications and activities of promoting brands or corporate identity; and support of universities, research, and other charitable institutions.

[53] Id. at 11–12.

or other professional services; contributions of IT equipment or used office equipment or furniture; use of company premises (i.e., meeting rooms or other spaces); and provision of free advertising space in a publication, on a website, or through television or radio.[54] When valuing in-kind contributions for reporting purposes, companies should include only the cost to the company to make and not the amount that the beneficiary organization would otherwise have to pay in the open market (e.g., companies donating products should value them at their average unit cost of production and not their retail value). LBG noted that in-kind contributions often present challenging valuation issues and urge companies to be conservative in their estimates.[55]

Finally, in addition to the direct input costs of community contributions, companies can and should assign a value to and report management costs associated with making such contributions including expenses associated with community affairs staff (i.e., salaries, pension and social security contributions, benefits, and recruitment costs); operational and overhead costs (i.e., phones, IT, travel, subsistence for business as a whole); professional advice relating to establishing, maintaining, and improving the program; reasonable costs associated with communicating the community program to relevant audiences, but not the costs of communications and marketing designed primarily to promote the company's products, services, and brand; and research costs.[56] Management costs should be calculated carefully and reasonably and, once again, companies should be conservative in their estimates to avoid challenges to excessive claims. Reporting in this area should be limited to cost incurred with managing the community program as a whole. For example, LBG advised that if managing the program is just one aspect of someone's job, companies should only count the proportion of the cost of that person that

---

[54] Id. at 13.

[55] Id. See LBG guidance on valuing discounted work (professional services); exceptional one-off gifts of property and other assets; foregone income/opportunity cost; gifts of product from inventory; pro bono work; social banking/universal banking; use of company premises/resources; and written down product or equipment.

[56] Id.

relates to time spent managing the program. Similarly, the entire cost of creating the company's sustainability report should not be included, but credit can be taken for the proportion relevant to preparation of the discussion of corporate community investment in the report. In addition, management costs should be limited to the costs associated with overall program coordination and communication, not time spent on specific projects, which should be recorded as a "time" contribution.

Why

The LBG framework provides an interesting opportunity for companies to describe and explain what drives them to engage in corporate community investment by allowing for activities to be broken out into one of three categories of motivation, each of which represents a dramatically different strategy and process: charitable gifts; community investment; and commercial initiatives in the community. LBG argued that having companies address "why we contribute" provides an indication of the strategic nature of the activity, shows the degree to which it is aligned with wider business goals, and helps companies understand the extent to which they are either driving their contributions *or* being driven by external demands and circumstances.[57] Companies generally engage in activities that fall within each of the three categories; however, LBG noted that there appears to be a trend toward refocusing corporate community investment programs away from relying almost exclusively on traditional charitable giving and moving toward an approach that incorporates a clear set of strategic objectives against which companies can assess their progress.[58]

Charitable giving, sometimes referred to as "grant making," has been a large part of traditional corporate philanthropy for a long time and was described by LBG as tending to be reactive in that they occurred as responses to appeals for help that came directly from charities or through requests from employees (including matched funding or payroll giving). Many of the instances of charitable giving tend to be short term, ad hoc,

---

[57] Id. at 14.

[58] Id.

or one-off contributions that companies approve largely because it seems to be "the right thing to do" and not necessarily because the action is part of a broader strategic plan or taken with an anticipation of a specific return to the company. Examples of charitable giving cited by LBG included sending cash or other resources to support victims of an earthquake, sponsoring an employee in their own fund-raising activity, a grant from a corporate foundation that is not linked to an overarching strategy or objective, and enabling an employee to undertake one-off or occasional volunteering or fund-raising activities during paid working time.[59] When engaging in charitable giving companies have generally relied on the good faith of the recipient to use the donation wisely, even in situations where the size of the grant is quite large, rather than imposing requirements on use that would facilitate assessment of impact and the performance and skills of the recipient. Such an approach appears reasonable in circumstances where the cause appears to be worthwhile and the recipient has built a positive reputation in the community; however, investors and other stakeholders, including community members, are being more aggressive about pushing companies to consider emerging alternatives to traditional philanthropy that have a strategic element, including critical measurement of outputs and impact, such as engaged or catalytic philanthropy or a "shared value" focus.

Community investments are generally larger than charitable gifts and are deliberately intended to be much more proactive and strategic than traditional charitable giving. Community investments typically occur as part of a program of a small number of larger-scale, long-term projects, many of which are structured as a partnership with, rather than a donation to, one or more community-based organizations. LBG explained that community investing should focus on addressing the social issue(s) that the company has identified and targeted as being relevant to both the company and the community in which it operates, and should be linked to a wider community strategy, measured and helpful to protecting the long-term corporate interests and reputation of the business. Examples of community investment activity provided by LBG included employees

---

[59] Id.

volunteering at a local school as reading partners over an academic year to increase levels of literacy; a technology company partnering with an educational charity to run STEM (Science, Technology, Engineering, and Math) workshops in schools to encourage take up of the subjects; a financial service company funding a charity that works with elderly people to fund money management classes; a technology company supporting community groups to provide unemployed people with online resources to look for work; and a drinks company working with an NGO to develop water conservation projects in water-scarce areas in developing countries.[60] Other characteristics of community investments mentioned by LBG included a major commitment of resources; linkage into some sort of systematic measurement and reporting of results; targeting to a specific stakeholder group; and related to or drawing on the core competencies and resources of the company.[61]

Commercial initiatives in the community were explained by LBG as being business-related activities usually undertaken by departments outside of the community relations function (e.g., marketing or research and development) to deliver community benefit while simultaneously supporting the commercial success of the company and promoting its brand and other policies.[62] Pursuing community and business objectives in this way can be a tricky proposition and should be undertaken carefully to ensure that the company's actions are not viewed with cynicism. LBG pointed out that the most common example of this type of activity has become widely known as "cause-related marketing," which are primarily marketing campaigns that also involve a contribution from the company to a charitable cause. Examples of this approach provided by LBG included a consumer goods company donating a tetanus vaccine for every packet of diapers sold and a retailer donating vouchers for schools to redeem for computer equipment in return for product bought. Another type of commercial initiative in the community would be a science or technology company providing funding to a local university to conduct research into a particular issue, such as finding a new treatment for a disease prevalent

---

[60] Id.

[61] Id.

[62] Id.

in the community, and then publish the results to improve the wider pool of knowledge relating to the issue. In this instance, the company derives reputational benefits and often a commercial proprietary advantage from proprietary legal rights to use the results of the research; however, the long-term value of such a project ultimately turns on whether it contributes to the resolution of a problem perceived to be important in the community.

When reporting on commercial initiatives in the community, companies need to be careful about including only those costs that directly benefit the community and not reporting the cost an entire marketing campaign or other commercial activity.[63] LBG pointed out that reporting on commercial initiatives in the community is often difficult given how close these initiatives can be to what would normally be considered part of the company's core business activities. According to LBG, "... the activity must be voluntary, not mandated by law or other regulation. It must have clear charitable purpose, with a net transfer of resources from the company to the ultimate beneficiaries."[64] Engaging in commercial initiatives in the community to create a competitive or other form of advantage is permissible as long as the size and scope of contributions is properly reported.

What

The LBG framework, drawing on categories that were intended to be broadly aligned with the main charitable purposes identified and recognized by national and international bodies and regulatory agencies overseeing charitable activities, allows companies to provide stakeholders with a picture of the social issues addressed by their corporate community investment programs and the relative importance of each of the issues. LBG describes the issues available for selection in reporting as follows:[65]

---

[63] Id. Tying the campaign to the sale or promotion of the company's products or services is not a problem; however, reportable costs should be limited to the community budget and not include items from line management budgets such as marketing, research and development, or human resources.

[64] Id. at 15.

[65] Id.

- *Education*: Contributions to schools, universities, or other organizations or projects that seek to promote, sustain, and increase individual and collective knowledge and understanding of specific areas of study, skills, and expertise. Companies may support formal "classroom" style education or more informal forms of developing knowledge
- *Health*: Contributions to hospitals, health trusts, and other health-related organizations that prevent or relieve sickness, disease, or human suffering, as well as promoting health and healthy lifestyles
- *Economic development*: Contributions to organizations or activities that promote economic development, such as regeneration or job creation projects
- *Environment*: Contributions to projects or organizations that advance environmental protection or conservation (e.g., through conservation of flora or fauna or through engaging people in activities such a recycling or other aspects of a sustainable lifestyle); however, the contribution must support environmental activity outside and company and corporate community investment does not include costs incurred by the company in managing its own impact on the environment
- *Arts/culture*: Support for institutions (i.e., theaters, museums, public galleries, etc.) that promote or protect arts activities, whether visual arts or the performing arts such as music, dance, and theater, and also includes activities or organizations that promote or protect "heritage" such as might be regarded as part of a country's local or national history
- *Social welfare*: Support to organizations or activities that promote or address the interests of those in need in society and facing hardship by reason of youth, age, ill health, disability, financial hardship, or other disadvantage
- *Emergency relief*: Contributions to disaster relief efforts
- *Other support*: Support for activities that cannot be classified elsewhere

Where

The LBG framework contemplates disclosure of the geographic profile of where the company engages in corporate community investment as a means for assessing the extent to which a company's investment in the community reflects its geographic structure. In other words, stakeholders are given an opportunity to determine whether or not a company is actually investing in the areas in which it is doing business. LBG allowed companies to determine the appropriate classification system to fit its own needs; however, for ease of benchmarking the default classifications for the framework were broken out into broad regional groupings of Europe, Middle East and Africa, Asia-Pacific, North America and South America.[66]

Collecting and Analyzing the Data

According to LBG, the "inputs" section of the LBG framework is by far the most straightforward and the most widely applied among companies that choose to report on their corporate community investment. One reason for this is that almost all of the data is available within the company, although the company still must have the capacity to collect and analyze the data in accordance with the reporting principles outlined above. LBG suggested that companies need to understand and set the scope of the data collection process (i.e., understand the company's corporate and community investment structures, what data is being collected and where that data can easily be found); decide which data collection system to use (e.g., internal accounting systems and/or third party corporate community investment/corporate social responsibility software); carefully train everyone who will be involved in reporting and analyzing the data with simple instructions and workshops; address time and resource challenges by providing a support function for the process and designing the process in a way that allows it to be completed within a reasonable period of time without unduly disrupting the day-to-day activities of the persons

---

[66] Id. at 16.

from which the data must be collected; and anticipate concerns by being prepared to refer questions to a higher authority, such as board members, and share the results of the process to demonstrate why the process is important and necessary.[67]

Outputs

The second part of the LBG framework focuses on "what happens" when the company makes its corporate community investment and looks at the outputs from the investment in terms of activities delivered, numbers of organizations and people reached, funds raised, and business-related activities generated. LPG emphasized that outputs are quantitative measures of what happens or what is delivered through a community activity, but should not be considered an assessment of the activity's effectiveness, quality, or value to either the community or the business (questions that are taken up when the LBG framework turns to the issue of "impact"). Measuring outputs from corporate community investment activities can be challenging because there are usually many possible things to choose from and companies are usually dependent on the organizations they support for collection and reporting of information. In order to bring some order to the process, the LPG framework provides a handful of crucial metrics in three areas: community outputs, business outputs, and leverage (i.e., additional funds raised or contributions levered from other sources).[68] It is hoped that these metrics can be easily adapted for a wide range of different activities and facilitate the capture of information that can eventually be used to assess impacts not only in the community but also within the organizations seeking to serve the community and the company itself, particularly the employees of the company involved in the activities.

With regard to community outputs, LPG wanted to focus on a small number of measures that could be readily applied across most community projects and activities and settled on the following indicators:[69]

---

[67] Id. at 16–17.

[68] Id. at 18.

[69] Id. at 18–19.

- *The number of people* directly *reached by or engaged in a community project* (e.g., the number of children benefiting from a school refurbishment or attending a course and the number of courses run, the number of people receiving vaccinations from a public health program, the number of teachers or nurses trained in a training program, or the number of trees planted in a community conversation project). Companies should only count direct beneficiaries and not others in the community who may have indirectly been impacted by the activity, such as community members who may have benefited from a reduced chance of illness due to vaccination of other community members but who did not receive the vaccines themselves. Similarly, only community members who use an arts facility in the community supported by the company should be reported even though it is available to everyone in the community and thus provides all community members with a new opportunity for well-being and education.
- *The type of beneficiary supported,* which gives companies a better understanding of the broad social groups, if any, to which the beneficiaries of a project or activity can be allocated. Companies are given great latitude in selecting the categories of groups that might be most appropriate for a particular project or activity.
- *The number of organizations supported* (e.g., when a company supports a reading/literacy program that is provided across many schools it should report all of the schools as supported organizations even if the company treats the program itself as a single project or activity).

The three indicators described above are most commonly used for reporting and benchmarking purposes; however, companies are obviously free to develop and track additional company-specific indicators that are relevant to their own set of programs and activities. For example, in addition to tracking the number of people attending workshops, the company will almost certainly keep a running total of the number of workshops held and this information can be used internally to set strategies for managing the costs of a particular workshop and increasing attendance at each workshop.

The indicators for business outputs are to measuring the extent to which community activities reach or engage with different stakeholders in ways that can influence the company's operational results:[70]

- *Number of employees actively engaged in the activity* (either on their own time or on the company's paid time)
- *Number of company's actual or potential customers/consumers actively aware of or engaged in the activity*
- *The number of organizations within the company's value chain (e.g., suppliers/distributors) that are actively aware of or engaged in the activity*
- *The number of other influential stakeholders, as determined by the company's own materiality assessment, reached,* which assesses active awareness of the activity by organizations that can influence, or be influenced by, the company's reputation (e.g., representatives of governmental and international agencies, NGOs, or "think tanks," corporate sustainability practitioners, academics, specialist consultants, specialist investors, or specialist journalists
- *The value of media coverage generated by the activity.* The final category of outputs, referred to as "leverage," seeks to iden- tify and measure any additional resources contributed to a community organization or activity that come from sources other than the company. LBG pointed out that while these are actually an additional input to a supported organization it believed that it was best to report them as an output because they resulted from the company's own contribution, encour- agement, or support. Three types of leverage are recognized in the LBG framework:[71]
- *The value of additional funds raised by or contributed to the community organization,* which includes the cash value of resources provided by employees through payroll giving; other employee contributions (either direct donations or funds

---

[70] Id. at 19.

[71] Id. at 19–20.

raised by employees); donations/contributions from customers; and donations/grants from other organizations or sources such as government or other businesses

- *The number of employees supporting a community activity in their own time that is supported or encouraged by the company* (i.e., the number of employees actively participating in events held or activities supported by the company that encourage employees to give up their own time to support a community cause, such as by participating in environmental cleanups or "fun runs" to raise money for charities)
- *The time committed by employees to activities in their own time resulting from the support or encouragement of the company*

One illustration of how leverage works with customers provided by LBG included a broadcasting company that created and sponsored a fund-raising "telethon" for a community charitable cause and underwrote the costs of producing and broadcasting the programming. In that situation, the amount of cash donated to the cause by the viewers of the telethon should be counted as an output of the leverage applied by the company. Another illustration offered by LBG was a company that offered customers to donate to an identified charity by paying an additional amount at the same time that they settled their bill with the company. The two illustrations provided support LBG's observation that leverage is often the first, and most straightforward, output indicator to measure and LBG pointed out that for many companies their abilities with respect to "unlocking funding for its charity partners that wouldn't otherwise be contributed" often leads to a result where the company's leveraged contribution values are higher than its own direct charitable contributions.[72]

LBG observed that measurement of output, much like the case with assessing the ultimate impacts of corporate community investment, is very different than measuring inputs. The information necessary to compute and report inputs is largely available inside the company, with the challenge being how to establish an efficient process for collecting the

---

[72] Id. at 19.

data; however, a good deal of the outputs look outside the company and this means that the company is reliant on the ability and willingness of community organizations to share information about their activities. In all likelihood the company will support a wide range of organizations and while some of them, particularly the larger and better funded charities and nonprofits, will have the capacity for providing detailed reporting, many smaller, local organizations will not. Companies need to have realistic expectations about measuring outputs and understand that they simply will not be able to measure all of the things that they would like.[73]

Potential issues with reporting outputs should not dissuade companies from engaging in what is otherwise a valuable community activity; however, it does make sense to identify the data that the company would like to capture from community partners in advance and create a data capture tool, such as a questionnaire, that can be shared with community partners in order to let them know the company's expectations. Companies typically prepare a template that includes questions on all of the LBG output indicators and then customize the template to fit a particular program and the company's specific strategic priorities for that program. Assuming that the community organization is willing, companies may even approach the data collection process as an opportunity to assist the organization in improving its own processes for evaluating the impact of its activities (e.g., identifying the number of persons reached by the organizational activities that the company has supported). Information received from community partners should not be accepted without question and companies should be cautious about data that seems to be out of line with what would reasonably be expected, such as claims of numbers of beneficiaries that far exceed the apparent capacity of the organization and/or the resources contributed by the company. If employees of the company have been present at any of the supported activities, they should be consulted on their own assessment of attendance, enthusiasm, and overall impact.

Corporate community investment has traditionally focused on inputs, both with respect to strategic decisions about how and where to invest and in reporting; however, by including collection of data regarding outputs into the process companies can take the first steps in demonstrating

---

[73] Id. at 20.

the value of the investment activities and improving the processes used to decide on what types of community investment activities should be supported. Simply being able to provide directors, executives, and investors with information on how many people were reached by a community activity supported by the company or how the company's investment of core resources enhanced the capacity of a local charity can have a dramatic impact on planning and budgeting for corporate community investment and makes it easier for investment proponents to create compelling business cases for additional activities.

Impacts

The third piece of the LBG framework—impacts—provides both challenges and exciting opportunities to transform the way that companies approach corporate community investment. LBG defines impacts as "the changes that happen to individuals, organizations and the business in the short or longer-term, as a result of a community activity."[74] LBG conceded that it is likely impossible to achieve universal agreement on what constitutes "change" or "impact" in this context, noting that account must be taken of both immediate short-term outcomes and broader longer-term effects and that there will be many who argue that measures of impact should be limited to difficult to achieve and measure "wider social changes" and that changes in individuals should be recorded in a separate category called "outcomes." LBG argued that it was suggesting a pragmatic approach that based on asking companies to focus on several key "areas of impact" against which both shorter-term outcomes and longer-term changes could be reported and seek to make a reasonable assessment of the depth and type of impact of the community activity on individuals (both people in the community and employees of the company participating in the activity), community organizations, the community environment, and the business of the company itself, with depth of impact being measured by the degree to which each of those groups or conditions were better off as a result of the activity.[75]

---

[74] Id. at 21.
[75] Id.

Community Impacts

Businesses, through their mere presence and by engaging in specific acts of investment of financial and other resources, can and do have significant impacts on the communities in which they operate. For example, companies provide jobs for members of the community and the wages paid to those workers can be used to buy goods and services from other local businesses, which boosts economic conditions throughout the community through the so-called multiplier effect. Businesses support local services through the taxes that they pay and their actions to demonstrate intent to follow local laws and regulations and/or engage in formal dialogue on local public policy issues. In many communities, businesses can buoy the reputation and community identity of their area by their presence. Community involvement by companies and their employees can touch individuals and groups throughout the community in a positive manner on a day-to-day basis. However, no company has limitless resources for community involvement and attention must also be paid to the expectations of other stakeholders. The pressures are particularly challenging for sustainable entrepreneurs, who must pick every project carefully and set the priorities of their businesses with care. As such, it is essential that companies ensure that their corporate community investment programs include processes and tools for measuring, and ultimately reporting, the positive impacts of those programs on members of the community and the organizations that the company has supported.

The LBG framework for assessing and reporting on corporate community investment includes three types of community impacts: impact on people, measured by both depth and type of impact; impact on the community organizations that received support from the company; and impact on the environment and environmental behavior. Effective measurement of community impacts begins with the community organizations that have received support from the company, either through grants or in the midst of partnerships between the company and the organization. The organizations are the experts on a particular area and will hopefully be collecting and analyzing information on their own that covers the same types of impact questions that are of interest to the company. Companies should disclose their intentions regarding assessment and reporting before the project begins and take steps in advance to figure out the best way to work with community organizations on collecting the information necessary for the LBG framework. In situations where the organization itself cannot or will not provide all the necessary information the company can reach out directly to beneficiaries with questions and/or attempt to track the actions and behaviors of beneficiaries over time. Third party collaboration of purported impacts and changes should also be obtained to the extent practicable. When assessing impact on community organizations, questions need to be asked directly to the organizations regarding the impact that working with the company had on the scope and quality of their services and processes and the profile of the organization in the community.[76]

With respect to individual beneficiaries of an activity in the community an attempt should be made to assess changes they may have experienced based on measures of *depth* and/or *type* of impact.[77] Measurement of depth of impact allows companies to assess the degree to which beneficiaries of a corporate community investment identified during the output stage of the framework are "better off" as a result of an activity using a scale with the following three points that represent distinctly different levels of change that might be experienced by a beneficiary:[78]

- *Connect*: The number of people reached by an activity who can report some limited change as a result of an activity (e.g., raised awareness of opportunities to improve literacy skills)

---

[76] Id. at 25–26.

[77] Id. at 21. LPG noted that the two different ways of measuring impact are complementary and that companies may choose to use one or the other, or both, depending on the aims and needs of their community programming. Id. at 24. Appendix 4 of *From Inputs to Impact: Measuring Corporate Community Contributions through the LBG Framework—A Guidance Manual* (London: Corporate Citizenship, 2014) includes examples of how to use the *depth* of impact scale and Appendix 5 of the Manual lists typical indicators that can be reported under each *type* of impact category. The Appendices may be useful tools for companies as they engage in strategic planning and business case development for their community-related activities.

[78] Id. at 22.

- *Improve*: The number of people who can report some substantive improvement in their lives as a result of the activity (e.g., actually able to read better)
- *Transform*: The number of people who can report an enduring change in their circumstances, or for whom a change can be observed, as a result of the improvements made (e.g., got a job as a result of improved literacy)

LBG provided several illustrations about how the three-point scale might be applied to activities focused on different types of issues. For example, a bank may contribute to social welfare by providing funds to a local charity that works with older people to provide financial advice. The output of that activity is the number of older people reached by the project and the impact can be determined by questioning those people in order to determine where they fall within three groups that include people that reported a greater understanding of financial management ("connect"); people that reported they are actively managing their finances ("improve"); and people that reported better financial circumstances as a result of using the knowledge obtained as a result of the project ("transform"). Another common type of corporate community investment is offering work experience placements to long-term unemployed people to improve their employability skills and support economic development in the community. For these projects, the output is the number of people provided placements and the impacts on those people can be grouped as follows: number of people reporting a better understanding of how to look for work ("connect"), the number of people reporting improved job seeking results (e.g., getting more interviews) ("improve"), and the number of people actually getting a job ("transform").[79]

Basic reporting of "depth of impact" includes numbers for "output" and each of the three categories. LBG pointed out that when companies review these numbers, they need to take several things into account. First,

---

[79] Id. For further details on how to use the depth of impact scale, see Appendix 4 of *From Inputs to Impact: Measuring Corporate Community Contributions through the LBG Framework—A Guidance Manual* (London: Corporate Citizenship, 2014), 33.

there is necessarily a lot of subjectivity involved in each of the categories of depth of impact and in many ways an assessment is more of an
art than a science. Second, the numbers recorded in each of categories
of impact headings are mutually exclusive (i.e., people who experience
a transformation are assumed to have also realized both connection and
improvement and are not also counted under those categories). Third, in
some cases the total number of people impacted will match the output
number, meaning that each person has been touched in some way by participating in the program; however, there will be situations where the total
impact number is lower than the total output number, which means that
not everyone who was reached by the program was also impacted in some
meaningful way by it. A good example of this situation is an "awareness
raising" campaign that may be seen by a large number of people but fails
to cause all of them to at least report that they have a better understanding of the issue to which the campaign applied. Finally, expectations of
the company regarding the depth of impact should be consistent with
the particular type of program and companies should not expect that
every activity will be transformative for all beneficiaries. For awareness
campaigns connecting with people and improving their understanding of
an issue is often the best result; however, employability campaigns should
have more transformative objectives since real impact comes from getting beneficiaries placed into actual jobs. LBG argued that results from
different activities can be added up and used to provide a program wide
assessment of the degree to which beneficiaries are better off as a result of
company support.[80]

In addition to *depth* of impact, the LPG framework provides companies with the option to track and measure the *type* of impact so that the
company can get an idea of the area(s) in which an activity has benefited
the people it has reached, information that can be used to build and communicate a picture of the way in which people are better off as a result of
the company's support.[81] The framework provides three broad categories
of types of impacts that can be used as reference points and it is possible

---

[80] Id. at 22.
[81] Id. at 23.

for a single participant or recipient to be recorded under more than one category with respect to a project:[82]

- *Behavior or attitude change*: Has the activity helped people make behavioral changes that can improve the person's life or life chances *or* has it challenged negative attitudes or preconceptions, enabling them to make wider, different, or more informed choices?
- *Skills or personal effectiveness*: Has the activity helped people to develop new, or improve existing, skills to enable them to develop academically, in the workplace and socially?
- *Quality of life or well-being*: Has the activity helped people to be healthier, happier, or more comfortable (e.g., through improved emotional, social, or physical well-being)?

LPG pointed out that each project is different and that all of the three categories may not be applicable or appropriate to every project; however, LPG argued that the categories allow for assessment of type of impact on a project-by-project basis and that the categories are broad enough for aggregation across projects so that the company can usefully report on the results of all of its projects. LPG illustrated its point with examples of two projects. The first one focused on financial literacy and involved working with 10,000 older people to provide them with one-to-one money management skills and debt advice. For this project, the two relevant types of impact were skills or personal effectiveness (8,000 of the participants experienced better money management skills) and quality of life or well-being (2,000 of the participants experienced improvements to their quality of life as a result of debt reduction). The second project was a partnership with a local enterprise charity to educate students about forming new businesses and encouraging them to develop

---

[82] Id. For further details on describing and reporting indicators of type of impact for each of the categories, see Appendix 5 in *From Inputs to Impact: Measuring Corporate Community Contributions through the LBG Framework—A Guidance Manual* (London: Corporate Citizenship, 2014), 34.

new business ideas. For this project, the relevant types of impact differed from those for the first project, although there was overlap. The project caused 6,000 students to experience an attitude change by inspiring them about the potential of setting up a business and led to improvements in skills or personal effectiveness in two different ways among 5,750 students (3,750 benefited from workshops on how to set up a business and 2,000 benefited from shadowing managers and employees of businesses). A company supporting these two projects would report the outcomes for both of them separately and also aggregate the outcomes falling into each of the parties and report that 6,000 people experienced a positive change in behavior or attitude, 13,750 people improved their skills or personal effectiveness, and 2,000 people improved their quality of life.[83]

The indicators in the LBG framework for impact on the community organizations that were supported by the company can be used to assess the company's contributions to increasing the capacity of the community organizations that the company supported and/or partnered with. For example, contributions can have a positive impact on community organizations by improving their existing services and/or helping them deliver new services; allowing them to reach more people or spend more time with clients; improving their management processes; increasing their profile; and/or enabling them to take on more staff or volunteers. The assessment scale includes four possibilities: no difference; a little difference (i.e., a negligible short-term change in this area); some difference (i.e., some demonstrable longer-term change in this area); or a lot of difference (i.e. significant sustained change in this area).[84] The importance of the contributions that companies can make in this area is often underestimated; however, businesses are often uniquely situated to provide community organizations with access to invaluable technological resources and the deep experience of managers and employees who can assist their counterparts at the community organizations in improving performance in marketing and communications, strategic planning, accounting and budgeting, and training.

---

[83] Id. at 23.

[84] Id. at 24.

The third type of community impact in the LBG framework measures how the company's support for environmental charities or projects resulted in either improvement to the environment through direct intervention or positive changes in people's behavior around environmental issues. With respect to impact on the environment, the key question is whether the activity has generated direct ecological benefits such as conserving land/water, protecting species, or improving biodiversity. When looking at the impact on environmental behavior, the key question is whether the activity has enabled people to conserve energy or water, or to make other positive changes in their behavior toward the environment. The scale is similar to that used for impact on community organizations: no difference; a little difference (i.e., a negligible short-term change in this area); some difference (i.e., some demonstrable longer-term change in this area); or a lot of difference (i.e., significant sustained change in this area).[85]

Business Impacts

In the LBG framework, business impacts include impact on employee participants and on the entire business of the company itself. With respect to the impact on employees, LBG is interested in the extent of changes in employees' attitudes, behavior, and/or skills as a result of participation in a company-supported community activity. Specifically, companies should look at three areas: job-related skills and the extent to which employees have improved in core, job-related competencies such as communications, teamwork, or leadership skills; personal impact including changes in areas such as self-confidence, job satisfaction, and pride in the company; and behavior changes including increased volunteering or becoming a more vocal advocate of the company. Information can be collected from survey tools and interviews of employees and/or managers who have observed the employee both during the activity and afterward and thus are in a position to provide an independent assessment of impact in the above areas. Employees can have measurable impacts in more than one of

---

[85] Id.

the areas and totals across the three areas should not be added together as this will likely lead to double counting.[86]

As for impacts on the business, the LBG framework attempts to assist companies in identifying the measuring wider business benefit from supporting and participating in community activities. The issue is obviously extremely important and the results will be an important piece of evidence in the company's deliberations regarding ongoing involvement in the community (i.e., how much and in what ways); however, LBG conceded that assessment of business impacts is probably the most challenging part of the framework. LBG recommended that companies look at the following areas to identify discernable business benefits from engaging in a community activity:[87]

- *Human resource benefits*: Has the community activity delivered improvements to the business through engagement, recruitment, and performance linked to community activity?
- *Improved stakeholder relations/perceptions*: Has the community activity improved the perception of external stakeholders, especially opinion formers, in ways that matter to the business, as a result of community engagement?
- *Business generated*: Has the community activity contributed to new business (e.g., increased sales tied to cause-related marketing, contracts won where corporate social responsibility performance is a criterion, new market opportunities)?
- *Other operational improvement*: Has participation in the community activity supported improvements in the operational capacities of the company such as increased resilience in the supplier and/or distribution chain?
- *Uplift in brand awareness*: Has the community activity generated a business benefit through an uplift in brand awareness (e.g., through increased media coverage or public awareness)?

---

[86] Id. at 24.

[87] Id. at 24–25. LBG members have access to a more detailed guide of how to measure business benefits from involvement in community activities.

LBG noted that each of the indicators assessed the degree to which awareness of, or engagement with, a community program by key stakeholder groups ultimately generated a discernable benefit to the business. For example, did a customer's awareness of the company's involvement in a community activity eventually lead to that customer purchase the company's goods or services? Have opportunities to be involved in community volunteering during their paid time improved the satisfaction of employees and motivated them to be more productive and reduced costly turnover? Has news of successfully company involvement in community activities enhanced the company's reputation such that the company is better positioned to win contracts from influential stakeholders? While LBG pointed out that companies could use a simple assessment scale to assess differences in each area (e.g., a four point scale running from "no difference" to "a lot of difference," which would mean significant and sustained change in an area), they could also use more complex measures such as estimating the cash value of the identified business aspects in order to calculate "business return on investment."[88]

A company's ability to identify and measure business impacts will be enhanced by effective planning in advance of engaging in community activities. When deciding on which community activities should be supported, companies should consider potential business benefits and then work with the appropriate functional departments to better understand the possible impacts and how they can be measured. For example, while it can be anticipated that employee volunteering programs will have a positive impact on employee morale, the human resources department should be involved in creating and administering the program and should ensure that the employees themselves have a chance to make suggestions about the best way to integrate volunteer work into their day-to-day duties to the company. A new volunteering program also needs to be aligned with other steps that the company may be taking to enhance employee satisfaction and companies need to find ways to allow employees to apply the new skills and confidence created from volunteering on other projects that are not part of the

---

[88] Id. at 25.

community involvement program. With respect to realizing increased sales of products and services from community involvement, companies obviously need the support of sales and marketing specialists and harvesting the reputational benefits from community involvement will require support from the company's marketing and public affairs teams. Finally, the opportunity to achieve broader business benefits from community activities means that corporate community investment needs to be included in discussions of overall strategy conducted at the board level and among senior executives.

While, as noted above, measuring the business impacts of community involvement is arguably the most challenging aspect of the LBG framework, it can be the most rewarding stage of the process and is certainly mandatory in order to develop a complete business case for a specific program and create a compelling story for stakeholders of how the company strives to make a difference in its communities and operate as a "good citizen" of the society upon which it is dependent. While some companies do attempt to complete detailed quantitative assessments of the return on investment for community activities, for most businesses, it is sufficient to concentrate on evaluating a few key programs with the largest investment or contributions using simple indicators for which information will be readily available. In most cases, impact can be readily identified without lengthy reports full of numbers; however, more detailed information will certainly be useful to making changes for future programs and activities. LBG also advised that companies should not feel that all activities should deliver a specific type of discernable business impact, such as increased sales of products and services. In fact, the real impact of many corporate community investments is felt among the beneficiaries and organizations within the community and the company will ultimately benefit from opportunities to operate in a community that is more sustainable due, in some small way, to the company's investments tangible and intangible resources in the community.[89]

---

[89] Id. at 26.

Best Practices for Presenting Information on Community-Related Activities

Companies can use the LBG framework described above as a foundation for clearly and consistently reporting and explaining their corporate community investment activities. Elements of a report based on LBG might include each of the following:[90]

- The total amount of corporate community investment through direct contributions from the company during the most recent year, with comparisons to investment in previous years to illustrate trends
- A description of how contributions were made during the most recent year broken down into the main input categories: cash, time, in-kind, and management costs
- A breakdown of where contributions were made during the most recent year, which could be broken out by large geographic regions for global businesses (i.e., Americas, Western Europe, Central and Eastern Europe, Africa and Middle East and Asia-Pacific) or international/national/local for smaller businesses
- A description of why contributions were made, generally broken out into three categories: charitable gifts, community investment, and commercial initiatives in the community
- A breakdown of what issues were addressed and what percentage of the contributions were channeled to a particular issue, with information being provided for each of the following major issue areas: education, health, economic development, environment, arts and culture, social welfare, and emergency relief
- Information, to the extent readily quantifiable, on impacts of corporate community investments inside the company

---

[90] For examples of reporting using the LBG Framework, see *From Inputs to Impact: Measuring Corporate Community Contributions through the LBG Framework—A Guidance Manual* (London: Corporate Citizenship, 2014), 8–9.

and in the communities (e.g., number of charities supported, number of volunteers, number of hours that were volunteered, and number of beneficiaries served; percentage of employees and community beneficiaries reporting a positive impact; and percentage of community members agreeing that the company is environmentally and socially responsible)

- Detailed presentations on particular activities or collaborations to provide stakeholders with more information and highlight specific achievements

Companies often rely on case studies as supplementary tools for presenting information regarding their community-related activities. Not surprisingly, there is no universal agreement regarding the length and content of case studies and companies may provide a short one paragraph description or include lengthy stories that extend for several pages and thus can significantly increase the overall length of the sustainability report depending on whether case studies are provided for each topic and/or location. The GRI Reporting Survey commented favorably on one company's approach to case studies that included detailed reporting and the following elements: the general background of the issues, initiatives, programs, or projects; the "challenge," which included the objectives and the anticipated and real difficulties in achieving them; information on "how we did it" or "how we are doing it," which includes an explanation of exactly what the company did during the reporting period to address the issue or carrying out the project/program; and, finally, a discussion of what the company expects to come out of the project/program in terms of benefits and impact to the community and the company.[91]

The GRI Reporting Survey took note of two other ways that companies communicate the positive benefits from their community

---

[91] Reporting on Community Impacts: A survey conducted by the Global Reporting Initiative, the University of Hong Kong and CSR Asia (Amsterdam: Stichting Global Reporting Initiative, 2008), 23. Case studies are generally integrated with the overall in-depth narrative discussion of the specific topic; however, some companies separate case studies into a separate section of the sustainability report or even distribute them as a different publication.

participation. One method was including testimonials from persons who have either worked with the company on community issues or benefited from the company's actions. While some testimonials are limited to a general expression of positive feelings, others are more focused and meaningful by providing readers with insights on the specific impact of the activities on the person delivering the testimonial. The second approach relied on the use of dialogues and interviews to present community issues with questions posed by community stakeholders and responses provided by leaders of community-related initiatives within the company. It is not always clear that the dialogue is occurring in real time and the value of the disclosures turns on whether the company's response provides insights on its managerial approaches and its assessment of the performance of its initiatives.[92]

---

[92] Id. at 23.

About the Author

Alan S. Gutterman's prolific output of practical guidance and tools for legal and financial professionals, managers, entrepreneurs, and investors has made him one of the best-selling individual authors in the global legal publishing marketplace. Alan has authored or edited over 90 books on sustainable entrepreneurship, leadership and management, business law and transactions, international law and business and technology management for a number of publishers. Alan has extensive experience as a partner and senior counsel with internationally recognized law firms counseling small and large business enterprises in the areas of general corporate and securities matters, venture capital, mergers and acquisitions, international law and transactions, strategic business alliances, technology transfers and intellectual property, and has also held senior management positions with several technology-based businesses. He received his A.B., M.B.A., and J.D. from the University of California at Berkeley, a D.B.A. from Golden Gate University, and a Ph.D. from the University of Cambridge. For more information about Alan and his activities, please visit his website at alangutterman.com.

Index

OTHER TITLES IN THE ENVIRONMENTAL AND SOCIAL SUSTAINABILITY FOR BUSINESS ADVANTAGE COLLECTION

Robert Sroufe, Duquesne University, Editor

- *Strategic Planning for Sustainability* by Alan S. Gutterman
- *Sustainability Reporting and Communications* by Alan S. Gutterman
- *Sustainability Leader in a Green Business Era* by Amr E. Sukkar
- *Managing Sustainability* by John Friedman
- *Human Resource Management for Organizational Sustainability* by Radha R. Sharma
- *Climate Change Management* by Huong Ha
- *Social Development Through Benevolent Business* by Kalyan Sankar Mandal
- *ISO 50001 Energy Management Systems* by Johannes Kals
- *Feasibility Analysis for Sustainable Technologies* by Scott R. Herriott
- *The Role of Legal Compliance in Sustainable Supply Chains, Operations, and Marketing* by John Wood
- *The Thinking Executive's Guide to Sustainability* by Kerul Kassel
- *A Primer on Sustainability* by Ronald Whitfield and Jeanne McNett
- *IT Sustainability for Business Advantage* by Brian Moore
- *Developing Sustainable Supply Chains to Drive Value* by Robert Sroufe and Steven Melnyk
- *Developing Sustainable Supply Chains to Drive Value, Volume I* by Robert P. Sroufe and Steven A. Melnyk

Concise and Applied Business Books

The Collection listed above is one of 30 business subject collections that Business Expert Press has grown to make BEP a premiere publisher of print and digital books. Our concise and applied books are for...

- Professionals and Practitioners
- Faculty who adopt our books for courses
- Librarians who know that BEP's Digital Libraries are a unique way to offer students ebooks to download, not restricted with any digital rights management
- Executive Training Course Leaders
- Business Seminar Organizers

Business Expert Press books are for anyone who needs to dig deeper on business ideas, goals, and solutions to everyday problems. Whether one print book, one ebook, or buying a digital library of 110 ebooks, we remain the affordable and smart way to be business smart. For more information, please visit www.businessexpertpress.com, or contact sales@businessexpertpress.com.

www.ingramcontent.com/pod-product-compliance
Lightning Source LLC
Chambersburg PA
CBHW061200220326
41599CB00025B/4547